Commercial SIGN
TECHNIQUES

Related books available from ST Publications

Commercial Signmaking Techniques

The ABC of Lettering
Gold Leaf Techniques
How-to-do-it Charts for the Screenprinter
How to Paint Watercolor Window Splashes
Professional Painted Finishes
Screen Printing Techniques
Sign Painting Techniques
Sign Structures and Foundations

Vehicle Graphics

Complete Guide to Truck Lettering, Pinstriping & Graphics
Pinstriping and Vehicle Graphics
Trucks

Sign Design

Mastering Layout
Sign Design and Layout
Sign Design Gallery
Sign Design Gallery 2
Sign Designer's Sketchbook
Signs, Graphics & Other Neat Stuff
Successful Sign Design 2

Classic Design

Atkinson Reproduced in Color
Atkinson Sign Painting
Henderson's Sign Painter
Modern Ornament and Design
1000 Practical Show Card Layouts
Strong's Book of Designs
The Theory and Practice of Poster Art

The Business of Signs

Computer Graphics Pricing Guide
Practical Sign Shop Operation
Screen Printer's Pricing Guide
Sign Contractor's Pricing Guide
The Sign User's Guide: A Marketing Aid
Signwriter's Guide to Easier Pricing

Step-by-Step

CINCINNATI, OHIO

Copyright © 1996 ST Publications, Inc.

All rights reserved. No part of this book may be reproduced or utilized in any form or by any means, electronic or mechanical, including photocopying, recording or by any information storage and retrieval system, without permission from the publisher, except by a reviewer, who may quote brief passages in a review.

This book contains material first published in *Signs of the Times,* world leaders in sign information since 1906.

Please direct all correspondence to:

ST Publications Book Division
407 Gilbert Avenue
Cincinnati, Ohio 45202
U.S.A.

Project editor: Bill Dorsey

Book design: Paul Neff Design

Photos of Larry Mitchell courtesy of Gerber Scientific Products.
Photo of GridView Aligning System courtesy of GridView Ltd.
Photo of SpeedPress tools courtesy of SpeedPress Tool Co.
Photos in "The Art of Graining" by Nick Simone; reprinted from *Professional Painted Finishes* by permission of the authors, Ina Brosseau Marx, Allen Marx and Robert Marx and the publisher, Watson-Guptill.

ISBN 0-944094-15-5

Printed in Hong Kong

CONTENTS

Introduction — 6

Section One: Vinyl — 8

1. Larry Mitchell, Tools and Techniques
2. Larry Mitchell, Applying the Film
3. Larry Mitchell, Registration and Repair
4. Larry Mitchell, Advanced Vinyl Application
5. Larry Mitchell, Specialized Vinyl Application

Section Two: Banners and Screen Printing — 50

6. Don Dozier, Making Banners
7. Mark Goodridge, Screen Printing a Real Estate Sign

Section Three: Wood — 70

8. Nancy Beaudette and Nöella Cotnam, Making a Multi-Dimensional Wood Sign
9. James Mitchell, Making a Blacksmith's Sign

Section Four: Paint — 98

10. Ina Brosseau Marx, Allen Marx and Robert Marx, The Art of Graining
11. Bill Jonas, Airbrush Sign Painting
12. Steve Chaszeyka, Pinstriping

Section Five: Resource Guide — 134

COMMERCIAL SIGN TECHNIQUES began as a simple idea: a step-by-step book on how to make commercial signs. Carrying out this simple idea proved more complex with questions of what techniques we would include and who would demonstrate them. We selected a fair range of signmaking techniques, not all, and the best people in the industry to show how to do them. Then the signmaking professionals took over. The experts photographed the techniques of their specialties and wrote the accompanying instructional text and captions. Some also shared gallery photos of similar finished signs, examples of what one can accomplish with these techniques.

This book is their creation. *Commercial Sign Techniques* is written by sign professionals for sign professionals. Readers can use this book to learn new techniques, combine some they know with others, and thereby expand their capabilities. Someone working primarily with vinyl on vehicles will find a complete section devoted to vinyl techniques, and also a chapter on pinstriping vehicles with paint. Banner makers may be interested in adding airbrushing or screen printing to their repertoire.

Commercial Sign Techniques is inclusive of many techniques, but is not all-encompassing. We chose these techniques because they represent the day-to-day needs of many commercial signshops. If this book is well received, we will publish another installment, covering more and different techniques.

In the meantime, we have this start, much credit for which is due to John Fischer, associate editor of *Signs of the Times*. John's suggestions of who should write each section proved very valuable, and his rapport with those sign professionals encouraged their participation. Also contributing were Tod and Wade Swormstedt, publisher and editor, respectively, of *Signs of the Times*. Tod, Wade and their staff's cooperation also helped to make publishing this book possible.

Finally, thanks to the project editor, Bill Dorsey, and all the contributors of this book, without whom there would be no book at all.

— *ST Publications Book Division*

TO CONTACT THE CONTRIBUTORS

Larry S. Mitchell
Larry Mitchell Productions
6720 McKinley Drive
Garden Valley, California 95633
Phone: (916) 333-2542
Fax: (916) 333-2803

Don Dozier
American Fastsigns, Inc.
2550 Midway Road, Suite 150
Carrollton, Texas 75006
Phone: (214) 447-0777
Fax: (214) 248-8201

Mark Goodridge
Screen Printing magazine
ST Publications, Inc.
407 Gilbert Avenue
Cincinnati, Ohio 45202
Phone: (513) 421-2050
Fax: (513) 421-5144

**Nancy Beaudette
and Nöella Cotnam**
Sign It
812 Pitt Street, P.O. Box 2A1
Cornwall, Ontario K6J 5R2
Canada
Phone: (613) 933-7447
Fax: (613) 937-3037

James A. Mitchell
Mitchell Signs
P.O. Box 12551
Ft. Wayne, Indiana 46863
Phone and Fax: (219) 456-1369

**Ina Brosseau Marx,
Allen Marx and Robert Marx**
The Finishing School
334 Main Street
Port Washington, New York 11050
Phone: (516) 767-6422
Fax: (516) 767-7406

Bill Jonas
102 Tenth Avenue
Belmar, New Jersey 07719
Phone: (615) 487-2168
Fax: (615) 487-3026

Steve Chaszeyka
Wizard Graphics
11511 Youngstown-Pittsburgh Road
New Middletown, Ohio 44442
Phone: (216) 542-0200

CONTENTS

1. Larry Mitchell, Tools and Techniques   12
2. Larry Mitchell, Applying the Film   18
3. Larry Mitchell, Registration and Repair   24
4. Larry Mitchell, Advanced Vinyl Application   30
5. Larry Mitchell, Specialized Vinyl Application 38

SECTION ONE • *Vinyl*

INTRODUCTION • *Larry Mitchell*

Larry Mitchell has built a highly successful career in vinyl graphics. He has managed this by first adapting to, then creating a few innovations in the industry. He believes that evolving with these changes is essential to growing a vinyl graphics business.

For Mitchell, if you don't adapt, you're standing still. Or worse, going backward. "I've had guys in front of me that just had an attitude. They had 15 years in the business, but essentially it was one year's experience repeated 15 times," he says. "They got to the point where, after a year, they figured they knew it all. Nobody could ever teach them anything. That's the worst attitude you can have in a creative, custom-product business like we're involved in."

It's 1976. Mitchell and a co-worker have cornered the vinyl-repair market in Memphis, Tennessee. The auto aftermarket, he finds out, is a good gig, and Mitchell makes a good living. In 1977 he starts striping vehicles with vinyl. He's so successful that the company he works for, Trim-Line, asks him to move on up to the east side of Oklahoma.

So Mitchell moved from the vinyl-repair business to the vinyl-striping business. The work was steady; business boomed in Oklahoma. Then one day, someone asked him to duplicate a roadrunner graphic from a license plate. If the request seems easy today, remember, this was 1979 BC, (Before Computers), the days of die-cut letters, pre-spaced legends and flat-bed plotters. In those days, vinyl was for seat cushions and record albums.

"No one would tackle the project, and I basically recreated it in colors of vinyl different than the plate colors," says Mitchell. "And they matched the stripe pattern." Consequently, Mitchell evolved further to graphic applications. "I realized that we could do anything with vinyl that we would with other processes as far as creating different shapes."

Thus, one of the original vinyl signshops was born. The first-generation business involved lots of experimentation. The stripe-and-trim business was a part of the mix, but so too was a business using pre-spaced lettering and die-cut components, all offset by hand-cut logo work.

The new development in graphic design logically led to the formation of a new business. Eventually, Mitchell sold his Trim-Line distributorship and incorporated under the name Vector Signs and Stripes. In the meantime, he attended various tradeshows and continued learning about his new-found craft. In Oklahoma, Mitchell had a hot business, but the winter weather was cold for an outside installer.

Florida, with its warm outside work, beckoned. So, in 1985, it was time to move to Mitchell's favorite part of Florida, the west coast in the St. Petersburg/Clearwater area.

Another big move occurred internally; Mitchell, who had been outsourcing his vinyl work, purchased his first CAS equipment and began wholesaling design and graphic work. For the first seven months, he and his wife worked out of a two-room apartment in St. Petersburg.

Too much work and too little space prompted another move to Palm Harbor, where he had a bigger signshop (read: garage) with a new name from an old idea: Trim Team.

At Palm Harbor, Mitchell could install with the speed of the best, and he could get a better price than almost anyone else. At truck dealerships, Mitchell could charge $125 for a custom-striping job that required 20-45 minutes. The dealers, who marked up his work about 300%, were more than willing to pay the price.

Mitchell's work was clean, and the designs were tight because he used pre-cut vinyl graphics, and he never cut into the paint job. The dealerships loved the markup of $389 to $429.95 per vehicle. "It was a way for the dealership to create profit in the negotiating range," says Mitchell. "They looked to distinguish their merchandise from what their competition had to offer."

Larry Mitchell
Larry Mitchell Productions

And Mitchell could deliver. He could also install with the best of them. One long high-paying day, he did 70 vehicles. Even so, Mitchell claims it was not the quantity of jobs that he went after, but the quality of the work. "I didn't hurt the other sign-shops," he says. "I didn't try to get their volume. I was doing distinctive, creative work so I could go and make more money off five trucks a week on that lot than the other guy could make off of 25."

The key to the higher prices is good design, believes Mitchell. Because he sold "exclusive originals" and not "cheap copies," Mitchell was able to charge two to three times more for his work than the competition.

He thrives by evaluating his own market. He doesn't sell against others; he sells what his market will bear. This marketing strategy, he believes, distinguishes him "from 95% of the trade."

"My whole marketing plan is not based on the cost of materials," says Mitchell. "Nor is it based on what the competition is charging. It's based on the perceived value of my work. A lot of guys can manipulate the striping as well as I can," he says. "But, when it comes to that part of the graphic that really catches the eye, I invested a long time ago in technology that would produce a much nicer, cleaner job."

Mitchell's first CAS system could produce work more quickly than what he calls "antiquated-production methods." His system was as easy to operate as an automated teller machine, he confesses. Nevertheless, Mitchell developed a knack of producing work others could not. He quickly learned to manipulate the equipment to his advantage. Others often told him a design (that he had just created), was impossible to do on the machine he used.

Despite his Palm Harbor success, Mitchell decided to move on again. (Apparently, a fussy neighbor did not like the daily UPS trucks at the house or his steady stream of customers.) Perhaps he had become a victim of his success. He needed, wanted and wished time to develop some ideas percolating in his brain. He had developed the ability to install a VOC-compliant spray-in-bedliner system for trucks that required no special spray booths or created any health concerns. Another Mitchell idea — a gold-plating system on automotive emblems — showed promise. Neither of these vehicle accessory items, Mitchell decided, was quite ready for market.

In 1993, Mitchell took out a lease with an option to buy on a place in Fort Pierce (located on Florida's east coast). As usual, Mitchell's new shop name was a variation on previous themes: it was called Signs and Stripes. In a matter of months, Mitchell had just about equaled the dollar volume he was doing in Palm Harbor. Fort Pierce might have been a place for Mitchell to stay a while, if the winds of fate (Hurricane Andrew) had not decimated the insurance industry's ability to cover his property affordably.

Fate intervened in other ways when Mitchell started a rough working idea of a new product: an interior auto-decorating system that uses a heat-transfer system to place cloth applications on headrests, seats, door panels and other types of upholstery. Mitchell called the process (and his subsequent company) Art-A-Tac™.

As is Mitchell's way, his new product built upon what he already knew. It required much of the same equipment he already owned; it dovetailed into industries he already had worked in (auto accessory and graphic arts), and it allowed Mitchell to outsource his primary source of income over the years: his design capabilities. The only difference with Art-A-Tac was a cloth substrate instead of vinyl.

Believing Art-A-Tac to be a "winner," Mitchell began bringing it to market. Developed over a few months, the process was unveiled in January 1994. Approximately 100 authorized dealers have signed up for what Mitchell describes as a "business in a box," including upholsters, sign and graphic firms, auto aftermarket companies, etc. A start-up kit, which includes tools and manuals, costs $795.

With a new business to focus on and an uninsurable business location, Mitchell once again sought another place in the sun. This time, he traded the beach for the mountains: Mitchell set up a rural shop, with the Sierra's as his backdrop situated a few hours from San Francisco — Garden Valley, California.

For Mitchell, moving on is a state of mind, a journey to excellence, a continual experimentation based on the need to improve.

As with almost anything worthwhile, the journey does not come without a major investment in time, determination and effort.

"One of the biggest problems with our craft is that people don't understand what mastery means," says Mitchell. "What they have to do. What price they have to pay. What mindset they need to have."

Now living in Garden Valley, Mitchell represents some specialized products, such as SignGold™, which he can distribute to his Art-A-Tac dealers. In addition, he is working on a book and has produced three videos.

Mitchell's five chapters will help you "master the principles" of professional vinyl graphics installation.

People from around the world know who Larry Mitchell is and call him constantly. Clearly, his reputation has spread. The world rests at the feet of a man who lives in the country and doesn't even have a sign out front.

TOOLS AND TECHNIQUES

TOOLBOX

1) Masking tools:
Mask dispensers, applicators, squeegees.
2) Preparation tools:
Tar, wax and grease remover; water; Bon Ami; towels; heat gun; and extension cord.
3) Layout tools:
Tape measure, Stabilo, 1/4- to 3/4-in. masking tape, 1/4-in. fine line tape.
4) GridView instrument.
5) Application tools:
Plastic, rubber and nylon squeegees; rubber roller; surface-conforming squeegee/rivet brush; application fluid; towels; Olfa knife and stainless-steel blades; and slitter.
6) Removal tools:
Heat gun, Li'l Chiseler, adhesive remover, towels.

Masking Tools

GridView Instrument

Peparation Tools

Application Tools

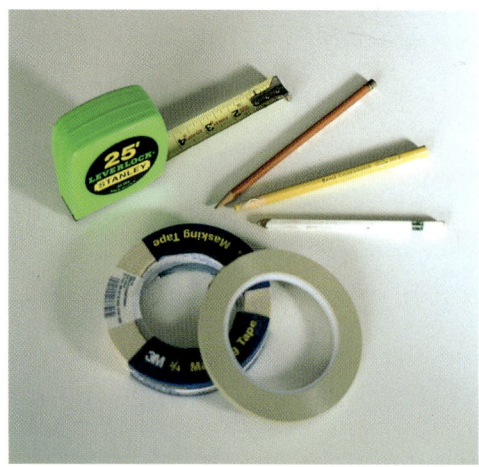
Layout Tools

Removal Tools

VINYL SELECTION

MASTER PRINCIPLE: *Use the right vinyl to meet the demands of the job regardless of cost. Substituting cheaper materials is a false economy.*

Use, environmental exposure and customer expectation will determine which film product to select. Keep in mind that customers shopping for lowest price will verbally minimize the expected usage for the vinyl-graphic product and mentally expect the longest usage. Select a product that will out-perform either expectation.

Manufacturing methods for vinyl differ and create inherent performance limitations. Calendered vinyl will not perform identically because of these built-in "genetic" boundaries.

These conditions outline the proper vinyl selection.

Condition 1: Outdoor usage, long-term expectation, flexible substrates (banners, magnetic signs, awnings, vinyl wheel covers, etc.), textured substrates (concrete, brick, stucco, "vinylized" canvas, etc.), compound curves, vehicle exteriors, exposure to UV, temperature extremes and petrochemicals (solvents, gasoline, finish products). *Select:* High-performance cast vinyl if one or a combination of these conditions exist.

Condition 2: Indoor usage, temporary expectation, flat substrates, protected from exposure to UV light, temperature extremes and petrochemicals. *Select:* High- or intermediate-performance calendered vinyl is acceptable as long as no Condition 1's are present.

Condition 3: 24-hour visibility. *Select:* Retro-reflective film products.

Condition 4: Easy removability. *Select:* Repositionable film products. Note: All films are repositionable and removable to the trained installer. Repositionable film's chief advantage is easier removability two or three years after installation.

Condition 5: Very short-term usage, easy removal, paint stencil. *Select:* calendered spray-mask vinyl film.

Condition 6: Backlit, high-visibility color. *Select:* High-performance cast translucent vinyl.

Condition 7: Very long-term expectations, resists solvents and graffiti, and holds up under high-UV exposure. *Select:* Ultra-high performance cast fluoropolymer film products.

ENVIRONMENTAL CONTROL

MASTER PRINCIPLE: *All environmental extremes are controlled by you.*

Vinyl graphics enable an installer to exercise greater control over the environment than inks, paint, gilding, etc. The ideal temperature range for installing pressure-sensitive or self-adhesive vinyl films is from 40-90°F (4-32°C). Under hot conditions, water is used to rapidly draw heat from the application surface. The application can be accomplished before the surface has a chance to reheat.

Shade is your friend on a hot day; the sun is your ally on a cold day. Static conditions can be controlled by using anti-static dryer sheets, a light misting of water, rubbing alcohol or application fluids.

MASK APPLICATION

MASTER PRINCIPLE: *Problems with the application tape or pre-mask will transfer problems to the finished vinyl application.*

Application tape is used for transferring graphics from the release liner to the application surface. Three common problems encountered when placing the mask over the vinyl are: distortion, wrinkling and overlapping the mask.

These problems will exhibit themselves in the finished vinyl application by creating bubbles, wrinkles and misalignments. Avoid these problems by using mask of sufficient width to completely cover the full height of the graphics, by using a mask dispenser or applicator that will give you control over the mask application, and by using proper squeegee methods when applying the mask. Mask dispensers *(see photo at top)* hold the mask taut and straight as it is pulled from the roll. A mask applicator *(see photo at middle)* goes one step further and applies the mask in a relaxed distortion-free manner.

The proper way to squeegee the mask is to first pass over the center of the graphic and then use short, overlapping strokes to the edges *(see photo at bottom)*. Stroke firmly but avoid pushing or bunching the mask.

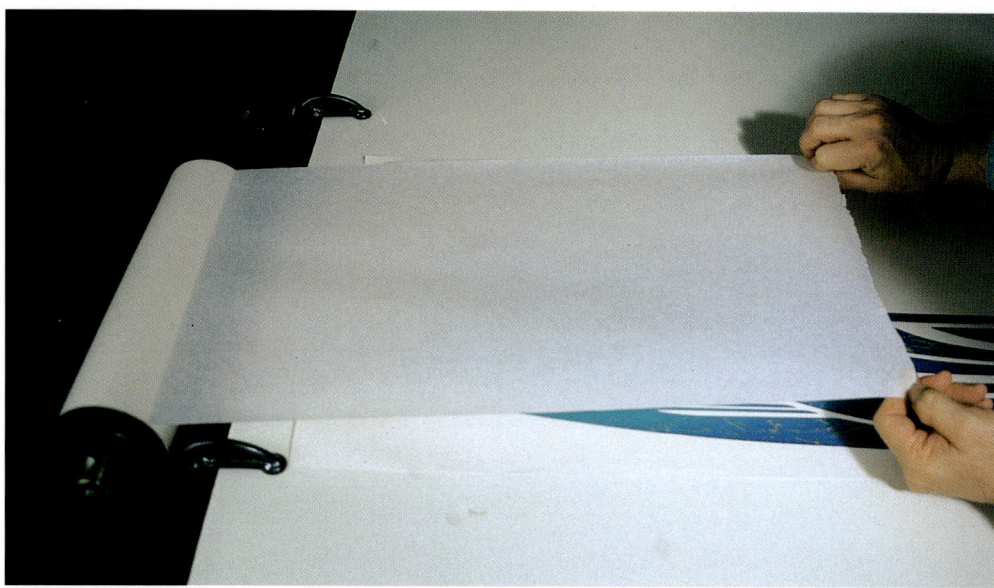

Mask dispensers hold the mask taut and straight.

Mask applicators free the mask of distortion.

Squeegee the mask in the center first, then use short overlapping strokes to the edges.

SUBSTRATE PREPARATION

MASTER PRINCIPLE: *Thorough preparation is the key to successful and long-lasting results.*

Preparation of a surface prior to applying vinyl is essential. Fortunately, it is a simple process that requires only a few minutes and the use of effective, yet inexpensive chemicals.

Two kinds of surface contamination have to be removed: petrochemical (tar, wax, grease, oil and gas residues, smoke films and polymer finishes); and organic (bug splatters, bird droppings, tree sap and common dust and dirt).

Petrochemical contaminants are quickly, safely and easily removed with automotive tar, wax and grease removers, which can be readily found at automotive paint supply stores. (Products that I have found effective are NAPA's Kleanz-Easy, Sherwin Williams' Sher-Will-Clean, and Ditzer's Wax and Grease Remover.) These products contain a combination of chemicals. A single solvent such as alcohol, denatured or isopropyl, is not 100% effective at removing the wide variety of possible contaminants. Stronger solvents, like reducers, thinners, acetone, etc., can damage the substrate material and often create an aggressive tooth that affects the repositionability of the vinyl adhesive. (Prep Sol is often recommended by vinyl manufacturers. It works, but I have found it to be oilier and harder to remove than competitive products that work faster and just as effectively.)

Organic-contamination removal requires water. Common dishwater soap can be added sparingly to make the water "wetter." In a pinch, spit works fine, too.

There are some instances where exotic removers may be needed. For instance, boats with fiberglass hulls may have leftover mold-release agents present. A reducer, such as DuPont 3812S, will remove this contamination. Just watch for the tooth effect this may give the surface. While this may be desirable for hand-gilding gold, it can cause loss of repositionability for a pressure-sensitive film product.

Exotic removers may also be needed when a surface has been exposed to acid rain. This has been a common problem on many new vehicles in recent years. The fallout left on the surface may have to be re-

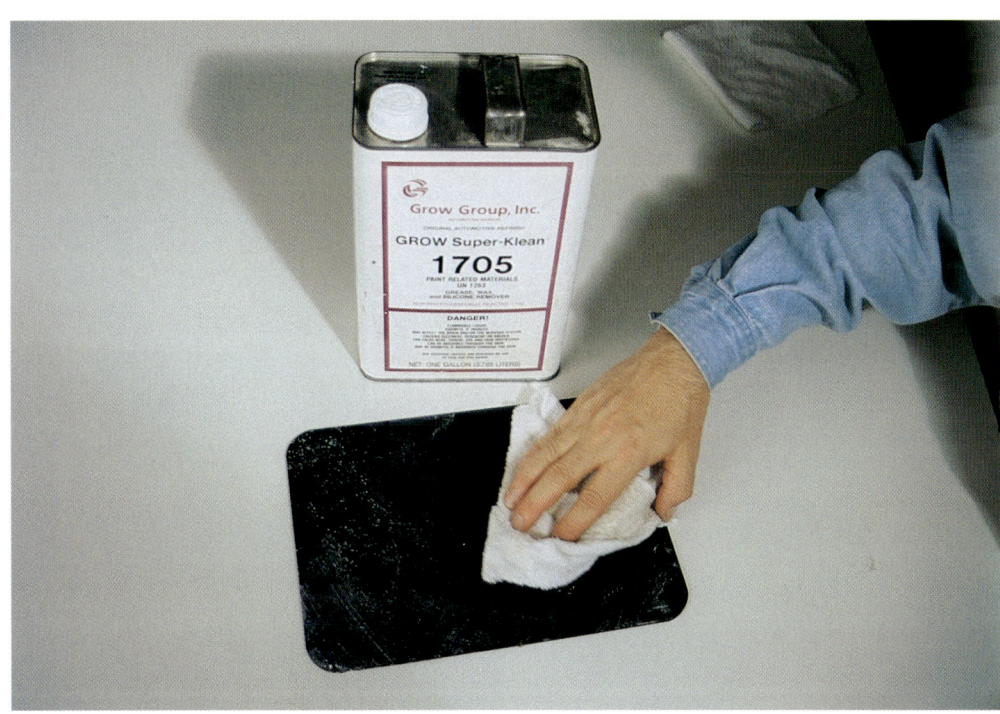
Use a second, clean towel to rub off the remover.

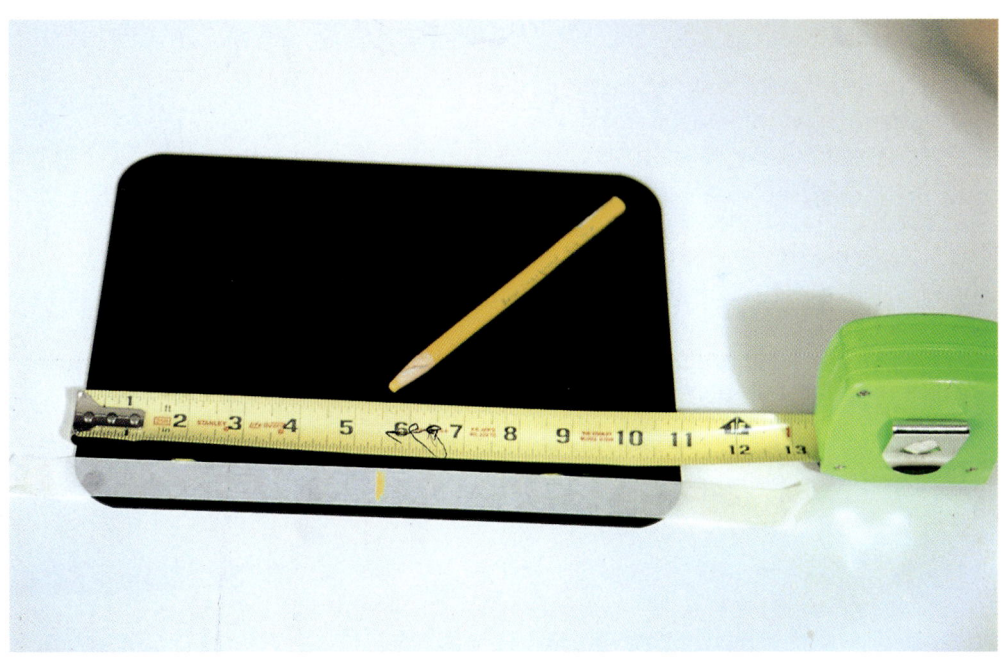
Mark two reference points between which tape can be tautly applied.

moved using a compound called Acidox and a buffing machine. The clear-coat finishes on modern vehicles sometimes resist the initial grip of the vinyl adhesive following prep with the wax and grease remover. In this case, keep a bar of Bon Ami (a soap with a mild abrasive) around. Wash over the application area with a paste from the Bon Ami using water and a clean towel. This will generally improve the initial "tackability."

Procedure is simple. With one towel, apply the tar, wax and grease remover. Use another clean towel to rub off the remover and any haze or film until the surface is clear *(see photo at top)*. If existing organic contaminants were not affected by the remover, then go back over the surface with water. If the surface was very dirty or dusty to begin with, you should go over the surface with plenty of water and then use the tar, wax and grease remover. Be as thorough as possible when cleaning any surface. The few extra seconds needed will save unnecessary problems.

LAYOUT AND POSITION

MASTER PRINCIPLE: Use the correct guidelines, then measure twice and apply once. Good layout begins with recognition of proper layout principles that can be learned from such books as Mastering Layout by Mike Stevens (available through ST Publications).

Another guiding principle is to correctly measure centers, margins and reference points. Most applications are made on a horizontal axis, whether this be the edge of the substrate, window frame, or, in the case of a vehicle, a dominant horizontal axis that is parallel to the rocker panel of the vehicle. Watch out for ascending or descending lines or body panels that have a pronounced convex contour. A very useful tool for layout is the GridView instrument, which projects light in aligning grids from an overhead position. This tool can significantly reduce layout time, especially in mass production jobs. A masking tape line can also serve as a quick position check before proceeding with the application.

After determining the correct position on the substrate, use a Stabilo pencil to mark two reference points between which a masking tape line can be tautly applied. This tape guide can be marked for additional placement guidance for left, right or center justification and used repeatedly if handled carefully.

The hinge method is commonly used to suspend the graphic above the desired area prior to the actual application *(see photos on this page)*. This can be accomplished with a separate piece of 3/4-in. masking tape.

A faster, simpler method is to use the pre-mask itself as the hinge by rubbing the mask along the top edge after the release liner has been removed, or, in the case of a larger graphic, by rubbing a vertical line through the pre-mask between two elements of the graphic, and then squeegeeing just the first part of the graphic, followed by squeegeeing remaining portions of the graphic into position.

The main principle to remember, when using the hinge method, is to be certain you align the graphic from the starting position correctly along the axis you are following. The starting position can be from either the end, the center or anywhere along the graphic, as long as your have properly centered or justified the application.

The hinge method suspends the graphic over the desired area.

A separate piece of 3/4-in. masking tape acts as the hinge for accurate graphic placement.

TOOLS AND TECHNIQUES • 17

Wet and Dry Technique

***MASTER PRINCIPLE:** Prtactice proper squeegee techniques so you can rely most often on dry application; wet application is your back-up.*

At times, wet application may be preferred even by the experienced installer (with certain environmental conditions). Examples include when the surface is very hot or the substrate has a lot of static build-up, as is often the case with plastic surfaces. Other conditions favoring wet application are: very windy, when alignment is critical, transparent or translucent vinyls are being used, the graphic is too large to easily handle alone, the vinyl is unmasked or the installer is a novice.

Wet application will go much faster and easier if a professional application solution is used instead of soap and water.

Experienced installers usually prefer dry application when conditions are favorable. Dry is definitely preferred with small letters or components, with striping and on compound curves or textured substrates.

1) Spray the substrate.

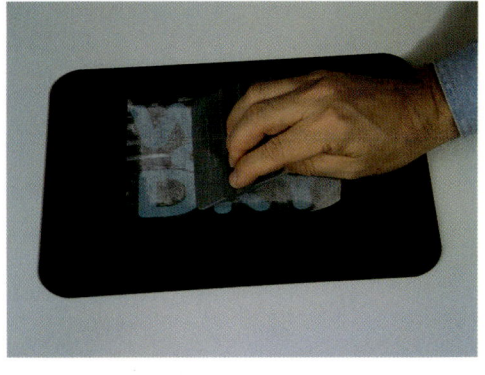

4) Squeegee properly.

2) Remove the release liner from the graphic and spray the adhesive side.

5) Spray the mask. Allow the penetrating action of the solution to soften the latex (30-90 seconds depending on humidity).

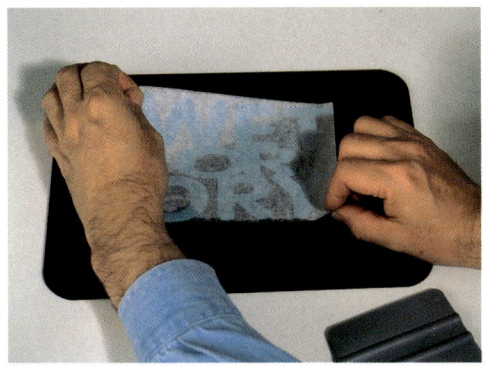

3) Position the graphic where you want it.

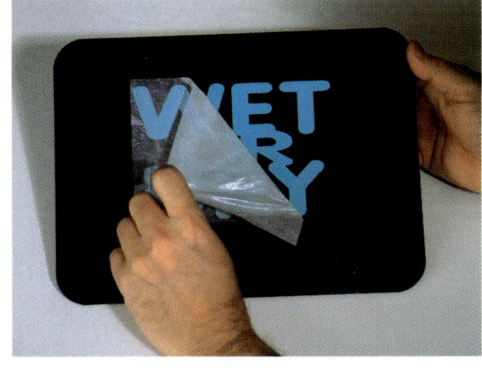

5) Spray the mask. Allow the penetrating action of the solution to soften the latex (30-90 seconds depending on humidity).

APPLYING THE FILM

Proper Squeegee Use

MASTER PRINCIPLE: Work from the center out with short, overlapping strokes to the edges.

Squeegee: Anything an installer uses to properly apply a graphic to a substrate. Your finger or the side of your hand can be used as a squeegee for small graphics or 2-in.-wide striping. Squeegees may be made from plastic, nylon or rubber. A wide, stainless-steel blade also can be used to squeegee application tape to vinyl graphics. One very special squeegee is the surface-conforming squeegee or rivet brush.

By far, the most common squeegee is a simple single- or double-bladed piece of stiff plastic that is usually 4 in. wide and comes in a variety of colors. This type of squeegee is typically used for applying graphics on flat substrates. If the blade is not rigid enough, or is worn or nicked, as is typical with "bondo" spreader-type squeegees, the application will often suffer from bubbles and/or wrinkles.

A nylon squeegee (typically gold-colored) is preferred for applying vinyl graphics to flat substrates because it does not wear out on the edge the way plastic ones do. If you have been using a squeegee for applying paper mask, you will notice a lot of edge wear, and it is best not to use that same squeegee for applying vinyl.

Unmasked, raw vinyl can be applied by using wet application and a rubber squeegee that slips readily on wet surfaces *(see photo above right).*

The surface-conforming squeegee *(see photo below)* is simply an inexpensive nylon paint brush that has had the bristles cut down to approximately 3/4-in. The bristle pattern should be fairly dense. This squeegee will press vinyl down into a textured surface or around the head of a rivet because it conforms to the contours of the substrate. More expensive rivet brushes are available, but the bristle pattern is usually less dense; the bristles are larger in diameter (which arc harsher to the vinyl); and they don't conform as well to textured substrates.

Unmasked vinyl can be applied using wet application techniques.

Specialized tools, such as this trimmed nylon brush, are needed for conforming vinyl to irregular surfaces.

Rubber rollers or brayers are often used for mask and graphic application *(see photo at right)*. When used correctly, these tools work well. However, the point of contact is generally broader than the edge of a squeegee, and consequently, it may be necessary to go back over a rolled application with a stiff squeegee to increase the downforce for a tighter tack to the surface. In addition, rollers also have metal parts that can accidentally damage the graphic or substrate.

The main difference between an experienced installer and a novice is generally the amount of time they've spent using a squeegee properly.

Whether wet or dry application is done, it is essential to use the squeegee correctly. Place the squeegee roughly 45° from the surface *(see photo below)* and use moderate pressure. Squeegee the center of the graphic first, then use short, overlapping strokes and work toward the edges. Keep the vinyl from making contact with the application surface; let the squeegee do the work. Repeat these actions with a slightly firmer pressure (it takes only seconds). Prior to removing the mask, use a finger to firmly burnish the edges of the graphic components. After the mask is removed, use a towel over your hand to reburnish the entire graphic. A friction sleeve over your squeegee can also be used to prevent scratches on unmasked vinyl. Or, you can lightly spray the vinyl and stroke the graphics with an uncovered squeegee. To summarize: use the squeegee correctly; let the squeegee do the work of placing the vinyl in contact with the surface; and avoid scratching the vinyl.

Rubber rollers or brayers are useful for applying vinyl graphics, but the point of contact is broader, which produces less pressure than a stiff plastic squeegee.

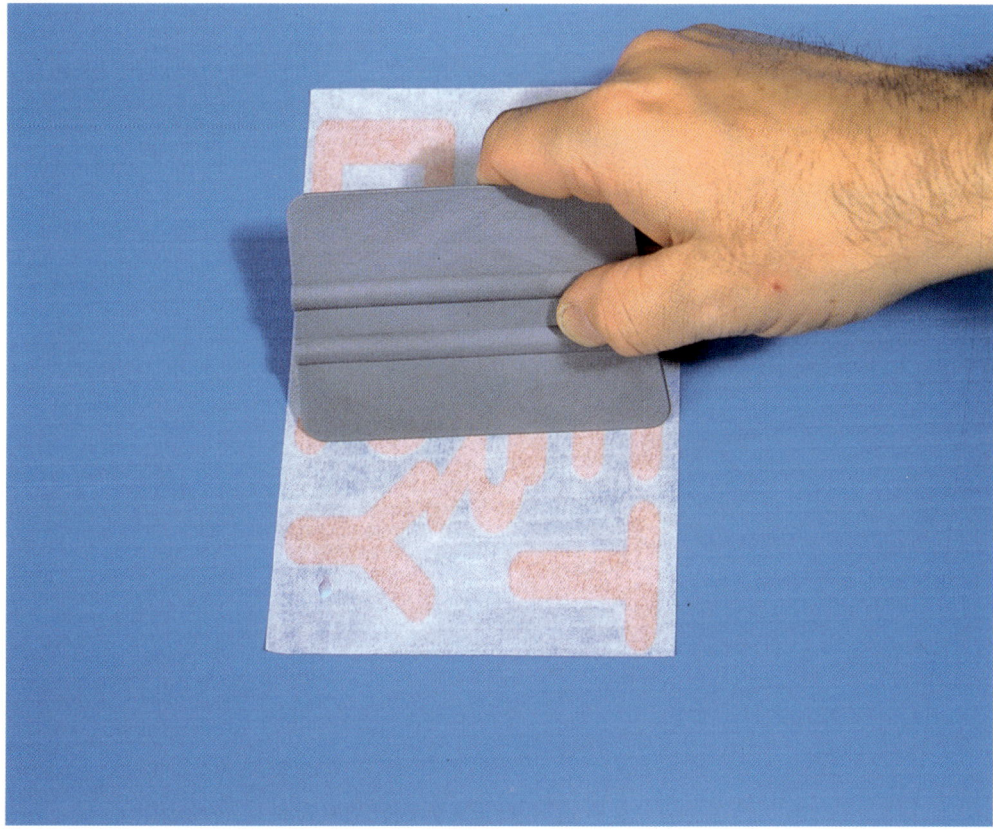

Squeegees should be applied at a 45° angle to the surface.

Squeegee Maintenance

MASTER PRINCIPLE: *The best applications are done with the right squeegee that is properly cared for.*

A squeegee with a bad edge is worthless. Do not mix up your mask-application squeegees with the ones you use for vinyl application. When the edge deteriorates, sharpen or replace it. A typical plastic squeegee can be resharpened by running the edge along the grip channel on another squeegee. But once the edge gets too worn or nicked, replace it.

Friction sleeves can be purchased to cover and protect the edge of the standard 4-in. squeegee. You can make your own from recycled Tyvek® envelopes or floppy-disk sleeves. Teflon plumber's tape, a towel or application tape also can be wrapped on the edge to help preserve it and provide slip.

Use the right squeegee for the right job. Textured substrates and compound surfaces require surface-conforming squeegees. When working with a heat gun or on hot surfaces, avoid melting your squeegee.

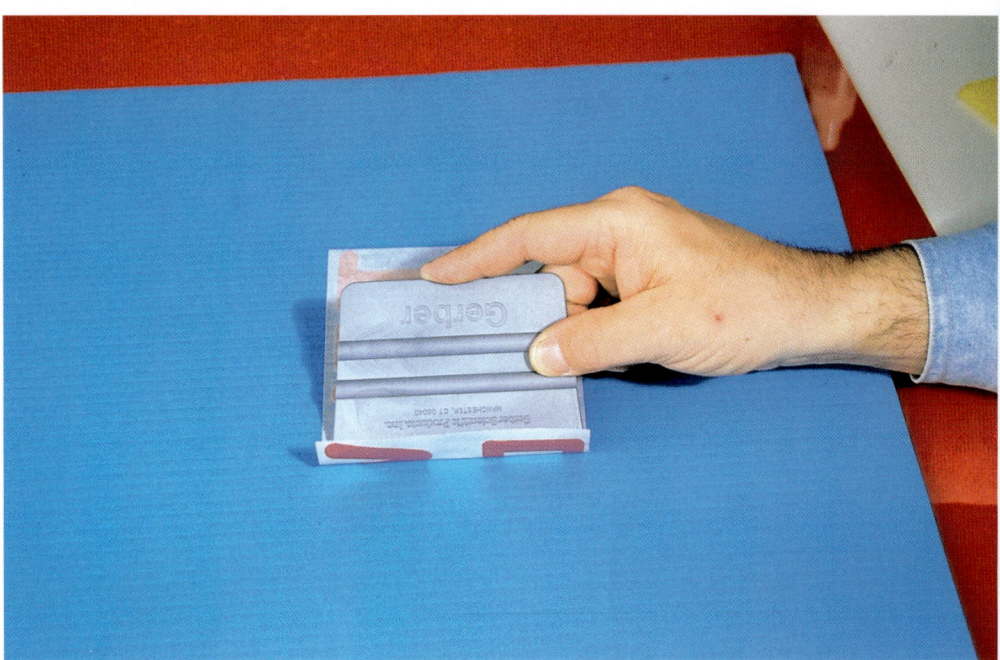
Squeegee the center of the graphic first, then use short, overlapping strokes and work toward the edges.

After the mask is removed, use a towel over your hand to reburnish the entire graphic.

Removing the release liner

MASTER PRINCIPLE: Remove the liner instead of lifting the graphic.

It is important to keep the graphic tight to the pre-mask until it has been firmly tacked to the application surface. If you try to lift the graphic with the mask, you may loosen the mask's grip on the graphic. A foolproof way to correctly remove the liner instead of the graphic is to lay the graphic face down on a flat surface with the pre-mask on the surface. Then, roll the release liner away from the adhesive side of the graphic, back over itself at 180° *(see photo below)*.

Calendered films have a matte or semi-matte surface that may adhere better to a high-tack mask. Textured film products will require a mask with a very high tack, which is available from some sign-supply distributors. Mask applied to textured films should be re-burnished prior to application because the mask has a tendency to loosen its grip if left in place for more than a few minutes.

Masks on smooth films tend to tighten their grip over time. Paper masks will generally have a higher tack than clear polyethylene masks. Striping can have either paper or polyethylene masks. The clear plastic masks on striping allow flexing and turning. The clear mask must always be removed after application. Leaving it on, especially on outdoor applications, will eventually ruin the stripe.

Store vinyl graphics away from heat and humidity. Do not get the release liner wet. Moisture will go through the paper and break down the silicone release layer in the liner, causing it to stick to the adhesive side of the graphic. Should this occur, use application fluid on any liner material that sticks to the adhesive and lift the bits of wet liner using the blade of a knife.

Pull the release liner away from the adhesive side of the vinyl at a 180° angle, folding the liner back on itself. This helps transfer the graphic to the pre-mask correctly.

Removing Application Tape

MASTER PRINCIPLE: *Pull application tape 180° back over itself, then re-squeegee.*

The climactic conclusion occurs when you remove the application tape from the installed graphic. If you have done everything properly to this stage, the graphic should be tightly adhered to the substrate and should be smooth without bubbles or wrinkles. Don't rush. Watch for loose edges and reburnish before proceeding with the pull.

If bubbles are present, simply puncture them at the bottom edge with the point of a knife or a pin. Then, push the air or fluid out of the hole with your finger or squeegee. Very small acne-like bubbles will generally disappear by themselves within a few days as the graphic goes through a few temperature cycles. Tiny bubbles will contract and make contact with the surface and not rise again. Just be sure to pop the big ones, or the adhesive will dry out, and the vinyl will crack in time.

Wrinkles should be prevented by following the recommended application procedures. If, however, you get a small wrinkle, you may be able to remove it by pressing from the interior end of the wrinkle out toward the edge of the graphic with the back of your fingernail. This action helps spread or redistribute and flatten the wrinkles. The only remedy for a severe wrinkle is to either re-do the graphic or carefully slice with your knife along the wrinkle and overlap the edges. The overlap is preferable to a raised, air-holding ridge of vinyl.

Do a final, quick inspection of your application. Give special attention to edges, tips and points; be sure they are tacked down. Clean the surrounding area of the substrate to remove smudges, fluid run-off, etc. Take photos and measurement notes in case you need to duplicate the installation in the future. Sign your work if you are proud of it and want the job to advertise for repeat and referral work.

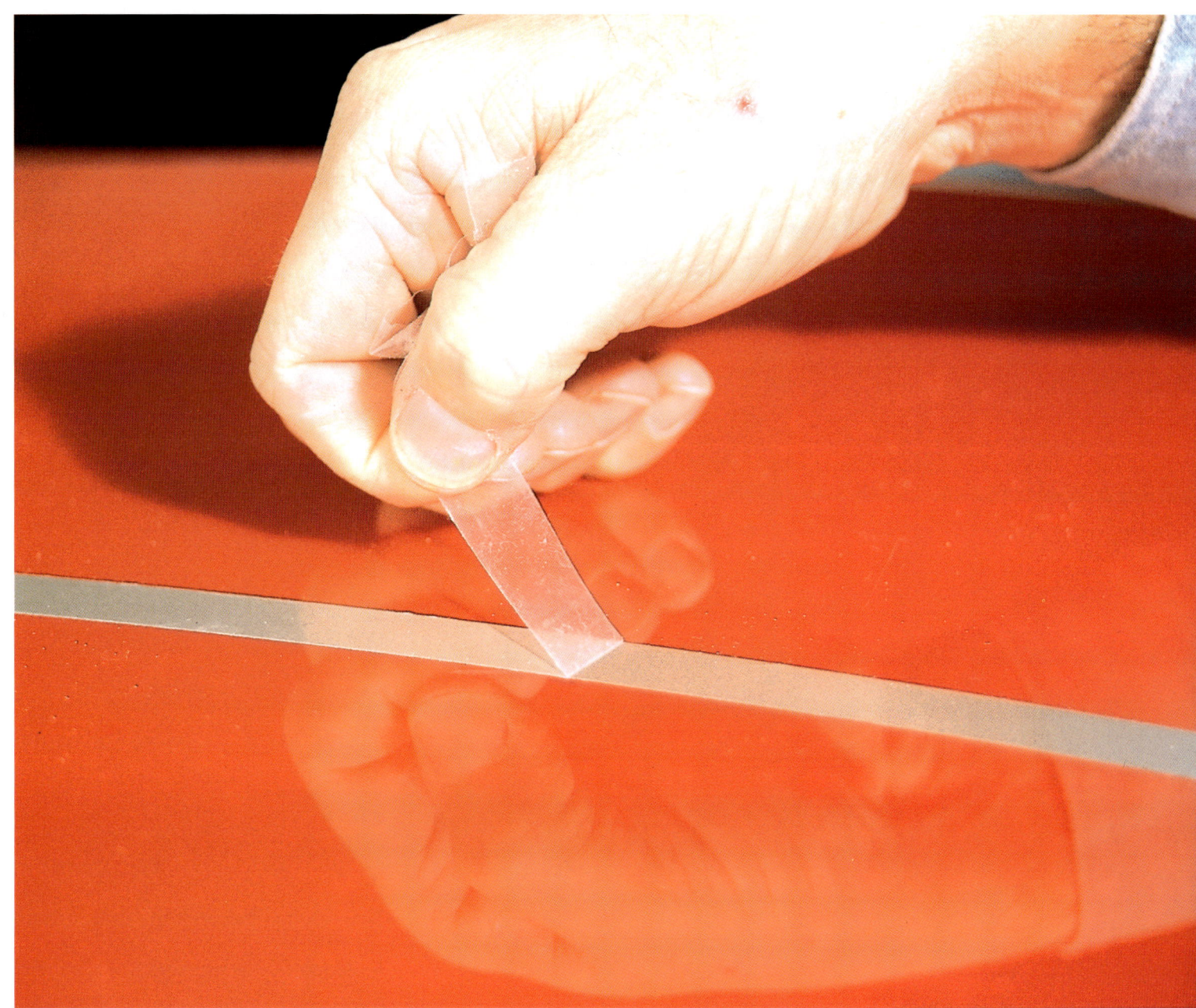

Clear mask on vinyl striping helps it flex and turn.

APPLYING THE FILM • 23

To remove bubbles in a graphic, pierce the film at the bubble's edge.

You can remove small wrinkles with your fingernail by pushing toward the edge to redistribute excess material.

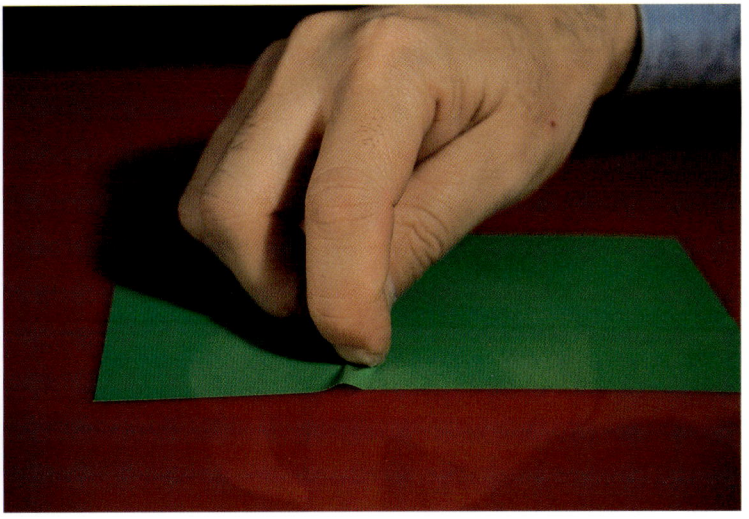
Then force the air or water out of the opening with your finger or squeegee.

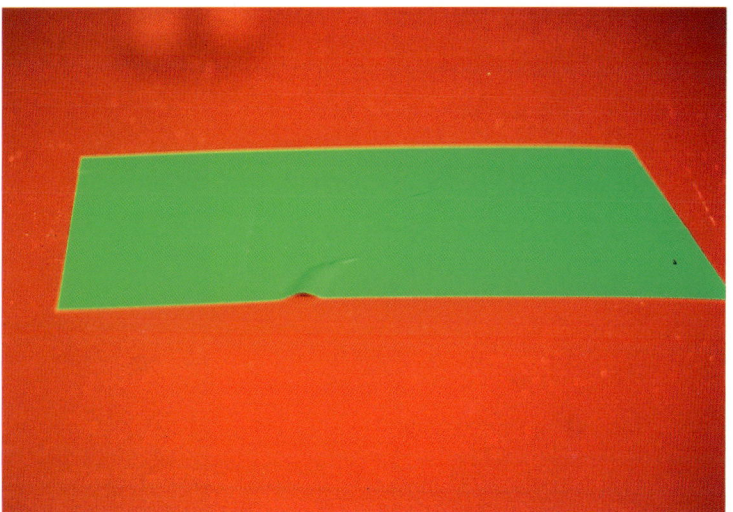
Severe wrinkles should be slit to overlap material if they can't be redistributed. This is preferred to leaving an air pocket in the vinyl.

Pricing

MASTER PRINCIPLE: Be sure to charge for your work in proportion to the value your client has received.

The value of your work is not determined by the cost of your materials. It is determined by the value of the quality, service, creativity and perceived benefits you have given your client. Use a standardized system of pricing as outlined in the *Computer Vinyl Graphics Pricing Guide* (available through ST Publications) to bring the authority of the written word to your pricing routine.

MASTER PRINCIPLE: Continued practicing of excellent fundamentals gives you the foundation for advanced performance and superior results.

REGISTRATION AND REPAIR

Vinyl application often requires using advanced techniques to manage difficult application conditions or more visually creative designs. Such techniques are needed for:
1) multi-component registration,
2) damaged or contaminated graphics,
3) detailed graphics involving dimensional perspective and paint effects,
4) extreme temperatures,
5) compound curves and corrugated surfaces,
6) striping techniques when cutting, turning and tapering,
7) textured or porous substrates and
8) easy, rapid film removal.

Multi-component registration

MASTER PRINCIPLE: *Registering multiple components is simply coordinating hand and eye movement with a relaxed approach to surface contact on the substrate or prior layer of film.*

Registration of multiple elements or colors of vinyl requires the careful coordination of your motions with surface contact. Premature contact may result in misalignment and ruined graphics. This need not occur if you first learn to relax with the materials. You should understand that contact does not necessarily mean bonding has taken place; you can release the film by quickly snapping the application away from the surface. The adhesive can make contact and still be repositioned, prior to any burnishing action. Possible exceptions might include smooth glass surfaces or plastic — situations in which wet application would be appropriate to avoid aggressive, initial attachment of the adhesive.

Wet application is commonly employed to help reposition graphics. However, a skilled applicator can use the aforementioned "snapping" motion to perform dry registration, thereby saving time and money. Generally, dry registration requires more hands-on practice with the film products until the installer is very comfortable handling and repositioning them.

Registration blocks or circles can also be used to align components or colors. This involves cutting small squares on each sheet in identical positions and placing them on top of one another. Although this procedure works, I rarely use it because of the time required to generate the registration shapes. Alignment of these shapes atop one another is as difficult as simply aligning the components with each other in the first place.

If necessary, I note or draw a portion of the graphics to illustrate proper spacing of the various components. But usually there is just one way for them to fit together, much like a jigsaw puzzle.

Work with only a portion of the "puzzle" at a time, aligning only the amount of graphic you can easily handle between two hands (about 12-18 in.). On larger or longer graphics, only roll back the 12-18 in. of release liner you are working to align. Once you've correctly positioned your first foot-long segment, the balance of the graphic should easily align section-by-section — providing you don't stretch or distort the graphic. (This is another skill you will want to practice until you have learned to relax with the film.) Note: be sure to stack colors in the proper order or sequence so the finished picture is correct.

Application tape or mask can affect your ability to position graphics. Although clear application tapes are easy-to-use, they may require a friction sleeve on your squeegee. In addition, they may impede the easy removal of the mask when wet application is necessary. Because they're translucent, paper masks can be easily seen through when the application comes in close proximity to the surface; this is particularly true during wet applications. Again, the close proximity required for this work means the installer must be relaxed and aware that surface-contact does not necessarily mean bonding.

Multi-component registration can be accomplished with a SpeedPress™ tool. Because this simple device is most easily used at a tabletop, it's generally found in shops. However, it is also usable outside the shop when graphics are being applied to a flat substrate. Using the tool may require two installers: one to hold the SpeedPress and another to do the application. Thin felt and/or magnetic strips adhesively mounted to the SpeedPress's aluminum frame will keep the frame from marring or scratching the substrate and create a hands-free steel substrate attachment capability. Attachable suction cups added to the frame will hold it on smooth plastic faces or glass.

When using the SpeedPress, remember that a flat, smooth surface is needed to lift the film from the release liner. The SpeedPress holds a clear pressure-sensitive film and you should position it over unmasked vinyl. Then press the film down on the vinyl with a rubber roller. The film will grab the vinyl and the release liner can be pushed off contact with the vinyl. Reposition the SpeedPress over the application surface and look through the clear film carrier to achieve proper alignment. Subsequent components or colors can likewise be transferred and aligned for proper registration. Apply each by using the rubber roller to press the vinyl adhesive into contact with the surface. Thus, multi-component registration is achieved using no mask whatsoever. The transfer film product that comes with SpeedPress comes in two levels of adhesion and can be used several times before replacement. Use a more aggressive transfer film when applying calendered vinyls than when applying cast films be-

SpeedPress Tool

Registering multiple elements or colors requires careful coordination of your motions with surface contact. Using registration blocks to align graphics is about as difficult as aligning the components with each other to begin with.

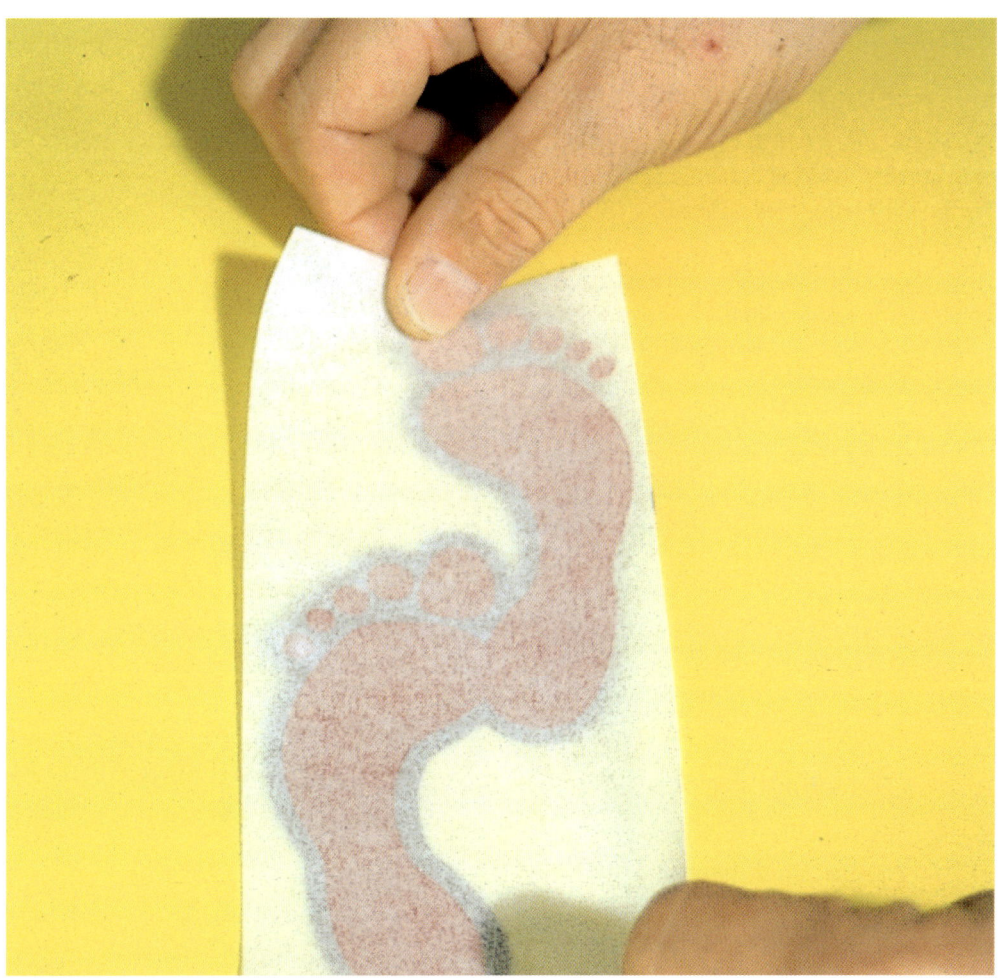

Attaining good, consistent registration requires practice and mastery of the basic application principles outlined in the previous chapter.

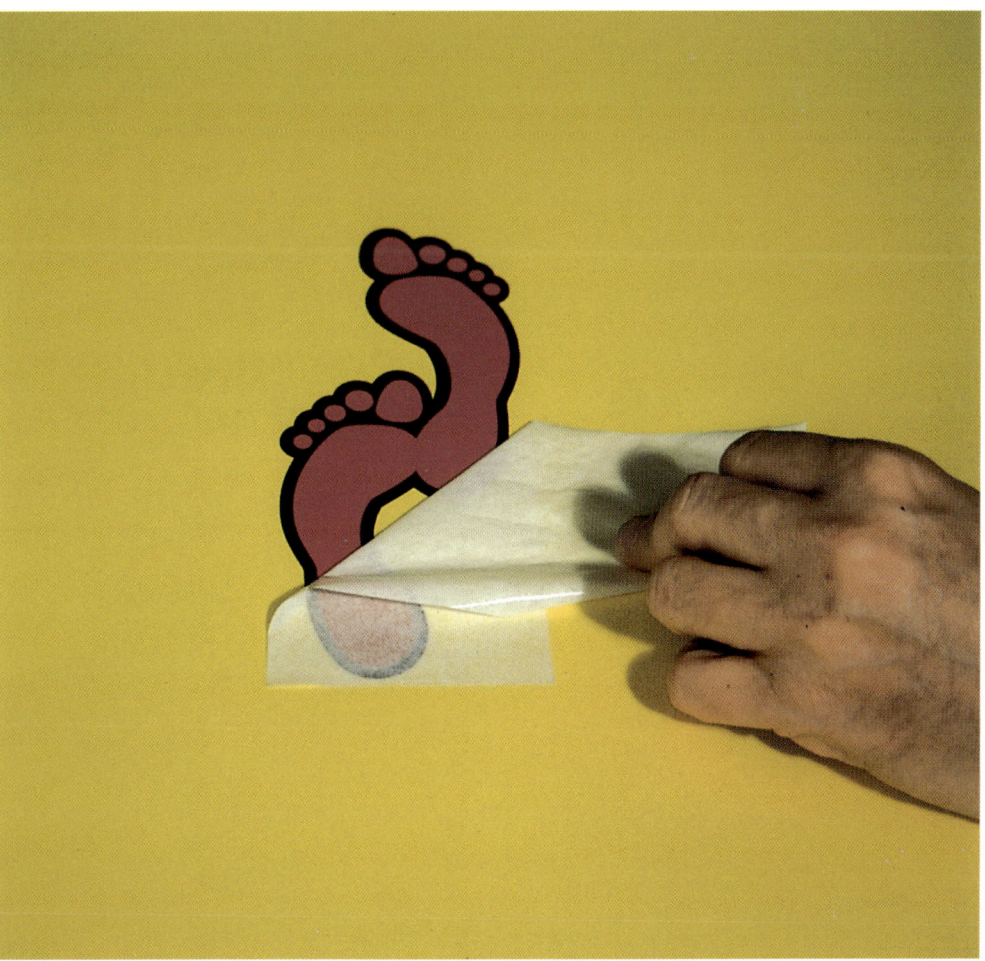

cause cast films have a smoother surface.

Repair and recovery methods

MASTER PRINCIPLE: *A vinyl graphic that has been damaged or contaminated can often be saved rather than replaced.*

Vinyl graphics are very forgiving in the hands of the trained installer. Should there be a blunder during your application, several methods can be used to eliminate the need to make all new graphics. These techniques can undo, camouflage, or repair damaged graphics. Even graphics that have been dropped in the dirt with the adhesive exposed can be saved.

If the vinyl sticks to itself when the release liner is removed, for example, it is often possible to remove the film by quickly snapping the vinyl loose. Practice with some scrap vinyl and you'll learn you can indeed separate vinyl that has made contact with its own adhesive system. This technique also works when one character folds over on another. For extreme situations where the contact is particularly aggressive, application fluid may also help. Put a little of the application fluid in the juncture of the adhesive contact area and carefully snap small portions at a time, or pull gradually if the vinyl is not distorting. Moistening fingers that are in contact with the adhesive side will help them avoid sticking to and

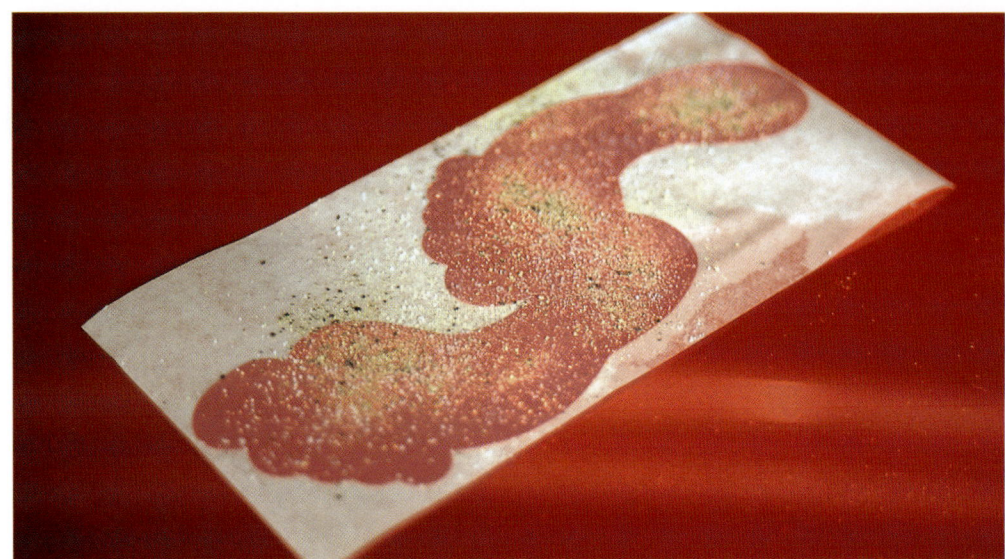

When a graphic gets dropped in the dirt, don't throw it away. Graphics are very forgiving in the hands of the trained installer, and there are several simple methods that can be used to undo, camouflage or repair damaged graphics.

Application fluid can be sprayed on the contaminated surface.

Then cleaned with a nylon paint brush.

distorting the film.

An application that has been scraped or torn may be repaired by replacing the damaged area or the component. If you choose to replace the damaged area, make a clean, surgical cut that you can replace with a smooth-cut patch. It is handy to carry some scrap pieces of the same colors you'll be installing, should this type of repair become necessary. To lessen the profile, the edge of your knife can be used to gently rub the edge overlap. Applying heat will further facilitate hiding replacement pieces or mending tears; it makes patches more moldable and allows you to stretch the edges over and under each other.

Patching may be a perfectly acceptable option as well, especially if the graphics are being viewed from a distance. Otherwise, just replace the smallest single-piece component. Prior to removing a damaged section, use a piece of application tape over it for tracing paper. Transfer the tracing by smoothly applying it to a piece of raw vinyl and hand-cutting the new component. Then, apply this field-cut component to the affected area. So that you can place the newly cut piece correctly in position, it is often helpful to mark the location of the damaged component on the substrate with a marker or masking tape.

What do you do if the adhesive side of a graphic gets dropped in the dirt? Don't throw it away! Wash it! Application fluid can be sprayed on the contaminated adhesive. Simply use a clean nylon paint brush to brush the dirt and fluid off the side of the graphic. Then, blot the edge of the application tape with a towel. Blotting removes the dirty solution before it can soak into the masking and cause de-lamination. This method also works when vinyl contacts paper and sticks to it. The paper can be loosened with application fluid and picked up with the point of a knife. Small bits can be brushed off with a nylon brush or a moistened finger.

If you notice a particle of dirt or sand under an application, rub it with the back of your fingernail. Gentle massage will often make it pop-up through the vinyl; the hole you have created will then lie back down and effectively seal and disappear. If a bug gets trapped under the vinyl (it happens!), you may be able to carefully release the vinyl's closest edge and extract the creature. Otherwise, make a small, clean incision and remove the insect with the point of your knife.

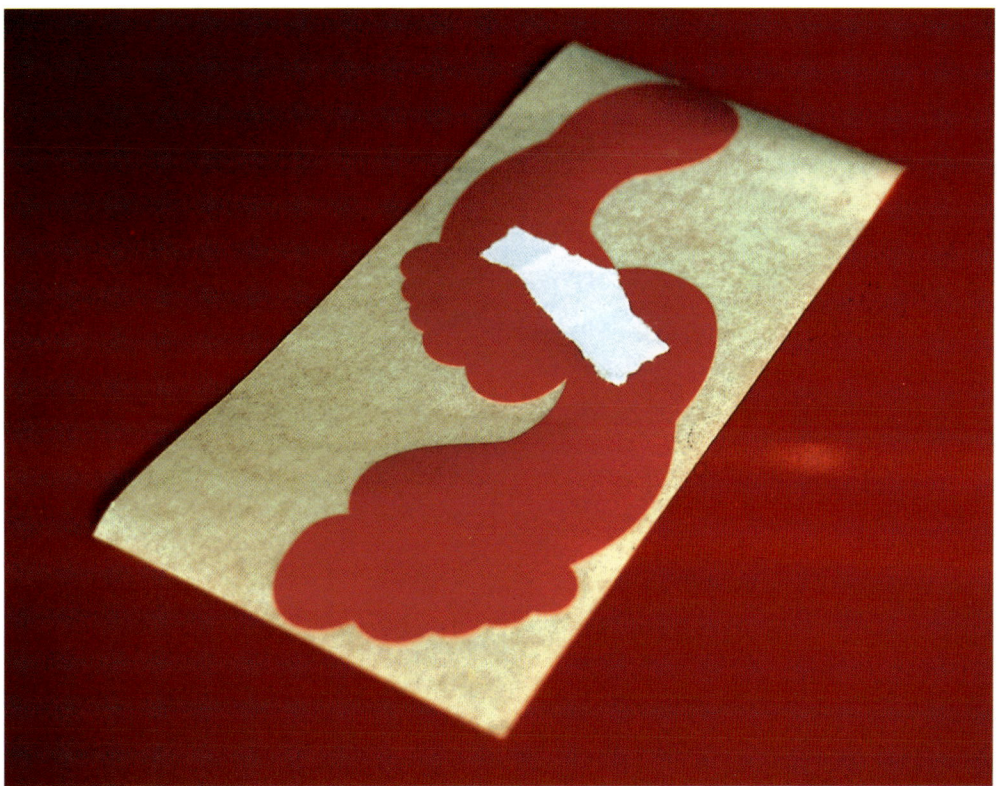

If a graphic is damaged by paper sticking to its adhesive, loosen the paper with application fluid.

Then, pick up the paper with the point of your knife. Any additional small pieces can be brushed away.

Dimension and paint effects

MASTER PRINCIPLE: Visual creativity and layouts are enhanced by thinking dimensionally to create illusions of depth and perspective. Blending the use of paint and vinyl quickly adds color, dimension and texture.

Using paint highlights and details on vinyl graphics can metamorphose the ordinary into the extraordinary. Highlights create texture, make colors visually realistic, and add body to an otherwise flat production. Learn from the creative artistry of painters by investing in some books on paint techniques and by following the work of skillful sign artists regularly featured in sign trade publications.

Outlining by itself increases contrast, but shadowing adds depth. Shadows make the primary graphic seem to project beyond the flat surface of the substrate. Skillfully applied, paint shadow techniques and newly developed shadow-effect films can make the primary graphic appear to float. Keep in mind that realistic shadows are made by darkening the color-value of the background, not by darkening the color value of the primary graphic. Depth illusion within a character itself is created by adding angular lines for a convex effect, curvy lines for a balloon effect, or a combination or wavy lines and blended colors for a horizon effect. Surface area on the character is created by chrome effects which cause an illusion of reflected light from that surface.

Additional perspective is created by combining elements that underlie the primary graphic. These are elements that have been reduced in size so they appear to withdraw into the background. Consider how real objects have a foreground, middleground, and often multiple backgrounds. You can make your production appear multi-dimensional by visualizing how various graphic elements spatially relate to one another. Closer objects must take on larger relative size, while background elements must become progressively smaller so they appear to recede into the distance.

Bringing elements closer together as you taper them toward a common point creates the illusion of distance perspective. Changing direction while tapering and narrowing creates the illusion of turning a corner and withdrawing into the distance. Distortion capability in your graphic production system can also be used to create additional dimensional perspective.

Textures can be created by using webbing sprays, sponge techniques, graining, smalt and marbleizing methods. Unusual paint or ink application devices such as lace, bubble-pack, plastic sandwich wrap, water bubbles, paint rollers, open weave papers or cloth, sand, cotton balls, toothbrushes, leaves from plants, crinkled paper, crushed egg shells, rice, crayons and candles and whatever else your imagination may conjure can be used to create a wide variety of special effects.

An excellent reference for achieving hundreds of different paint effects is Jean Drysdale Green's *ArtEffects*, published by Watson-Guptill Publications, New York.

Be sure to use paints or inks that will bond well with the vinyl. Various brands are available and experimentation is encouraged. Some products will last longer than others. If long-term exposure is expected for painted graphics, compatible clear-coating products should be employed. It may also be necessary to periodically reapply this clear-coating for maintenance purposes. In addition to their exposure-protection capabilities, some clear-coat products make vinyl more enamel-receptive (for example, Butch Anton's Sunscreen Clear). Regardless of the chemical product(s) you choose to use, test for suitability, follow manufacturer's directions, and exercise appropriate health and safety precautions.

Stenciling is another way to effectively use paint and vinyl products. Spray-mask stencil material used in conjunction with vinyl application quickly blends the two media. To block-out or protect the vinyl from paint application, application tape or mask can also be used. Computer-cut mask applied over enamel-receptive clear vinyl produces an easy-to-use paint stencil for the vinyl. This becomes an easy-to-install, painted graphic that is also easily removed down-the-road.

Modern color imaging technologies such as the Gerber EDGE™ and 3M Scotchprint™ make it possible to create multi-color, multi-dimensional, and texture-effect productions on one layer of vinyl while greatly reducing cutting, weeding, and application times. Photo-realism is achievable as well. Advances are continuing in this field and vinyl graphics will continue to increase in value as durability, creative expression, and ease-of-use improves.

REGISTRATION AND REPAIR • 29

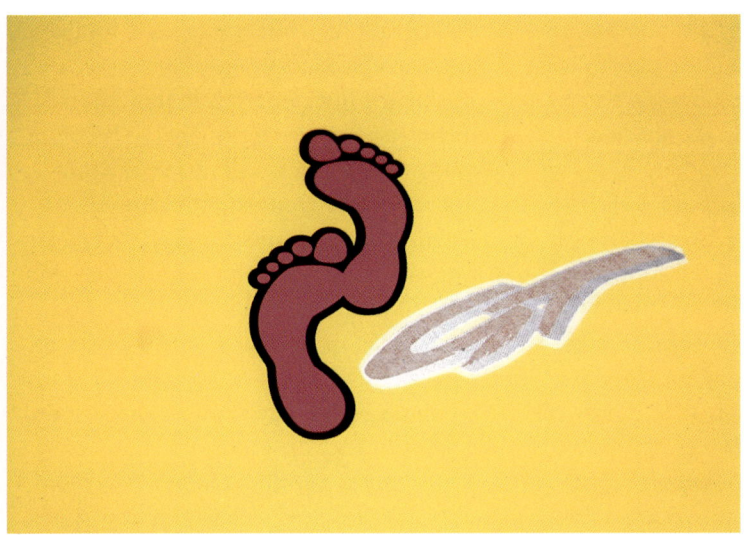

By understanding what viewers "see," you can blend paint and vinyl to create multi-dimensional effects.

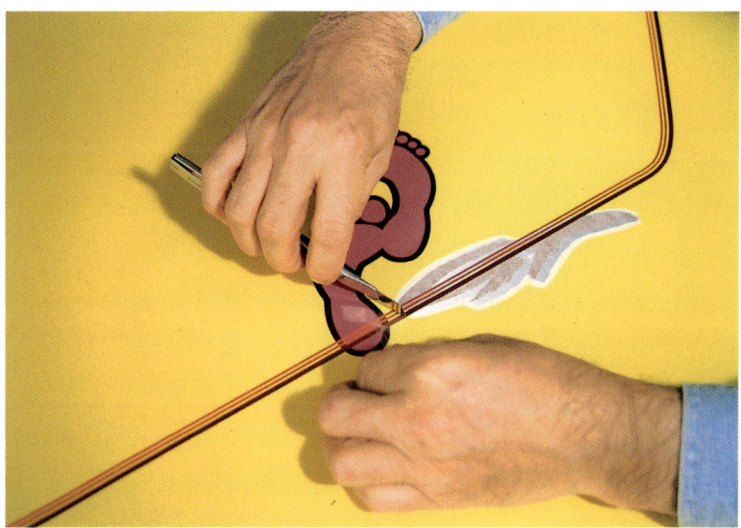

Notice how the vinyl stripe is laid over the feet graphic and the pre-masked "GT" graphic.

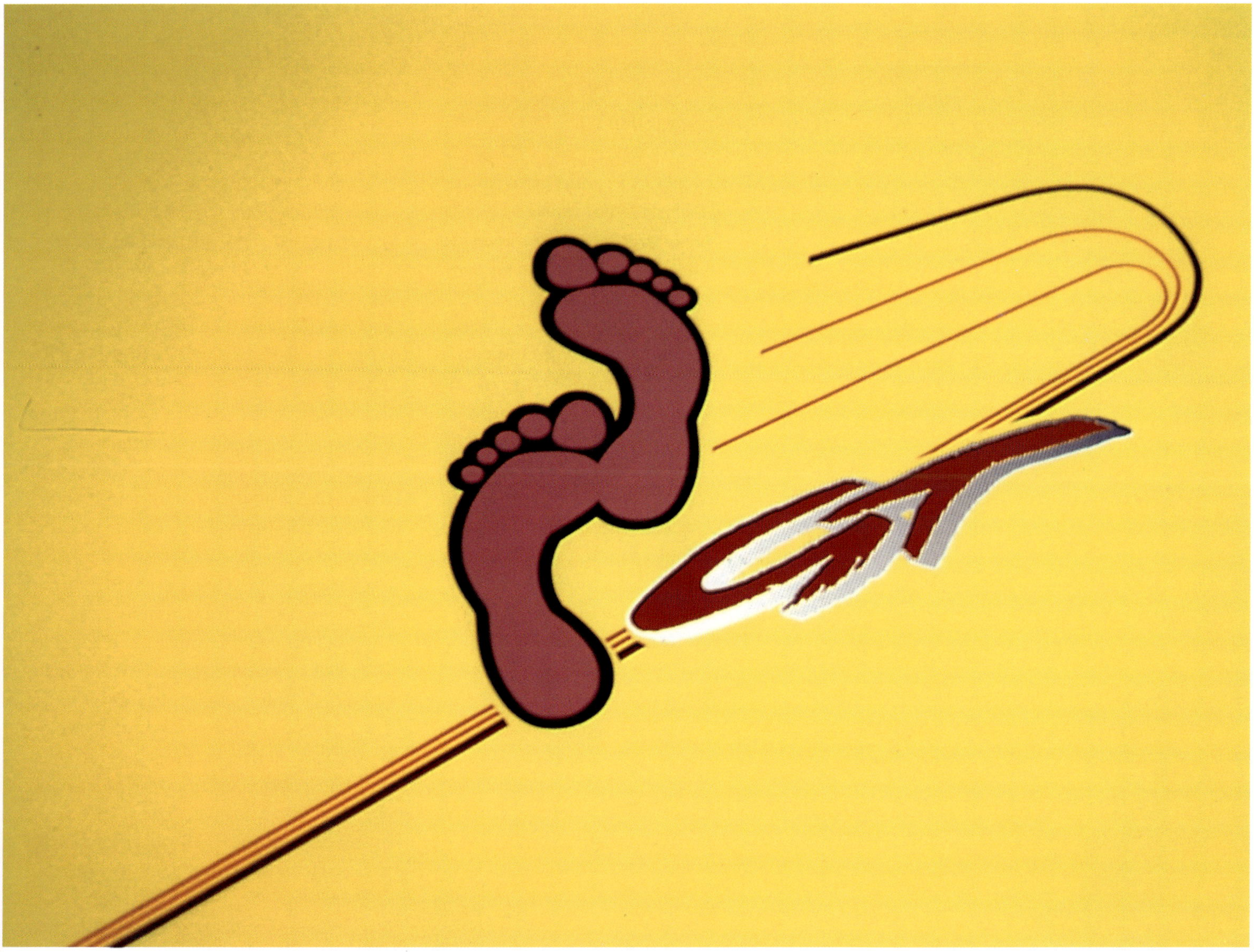

By cutting the strip around the graphics, it appears to withdraw into the background.

ADVANCED VINYL APPLICATION

When using vinyl, one often faces difficult application conditions or more visually creative designs, both of which require using advanced vinyl techniques. Three important techniques — multi-component registration, damaged or contaminated graphics and detailed graphics involving dimensional perspective and paint effects — were discussed at length in the previous chapter. The handling of extreme temperatures, compound curves and corrugated surfaces, striping techniques when cutting, turning and tapering, textured or porous substrates and easy, rapid film removal are the foci of this chapter. Specialized vinyl techniques will be discussed in the next chapter.

Temperature extremes

MASTER PRINCIPLE: Vinyl graphics can be installed within a broad temperature range because you control the vinyl and substrate temperatures.

A discussion of temperature extremes may seem to be an academic explanation to those who always work in the temperature-controlled environment of a signshop or garage. But sooner or later you will need to accomplish these types of applications outside the shop in less than ideal conditions.

Vinyl graphics can be installed on the hood of a black car at noon with the sun directly overhead. They can be installed on the same car in the shade on a sub-freezing day — even after you have chipped ice from the vehicle. How? By using methods for quickly cooling or heating the surface and the vinyl prior to application.

If applying vinyl in the heat, use a water or alcohol rinse to cool the hot surface rapidly. (Application fluid accomplishes the same cooling action, but the evaporation process makes using such expensive fluids cost-prohibitive. Instead, use application fluid after you've achieved the "cool-down.") Once the surface is cool or neutral to the touch, finish the application quickly before it re-heats. Blocking the sun is also desirable; if possible, put the surface and the graphics themselves in the shade or under a tarp.

Conversely, cold surfaces should be moved into the sun. A heating tool should also be used to warm both the application areas and the graphics. Suitable tools include heat guns and gas-powered torches. Torches are especially useful for larger surface areas, but require more time. For overall safety, speed and spot focusing, I prefer a heat gun. If you choose to use one as well, keep it moving around the surface; don't linger in one spot and don't get too close to the surface. If you point a hot tool at anything very long, you will burn, melt or cook it. Finally, do not lay a hot tool against anything that could be damaged by the contact.

Curves and corrugation

MASTER PRINCIPLE: High performance cast vinyl will conform to and remain on compound curves and corrugated surfaces when you use the right methods and stay within the performance capabilities of the film.

Try this experiment. You will need two samples of high-performance cast vinyl 1/2-in. wide and 6 in. long. Grab both ends of one of the sample pieces. Stretch. See how much longer you make the sample before it breaks. A sample whose temperature is cold or neutral will usually break after only 1/4-1/2 of an inch.

Now warm the other sample with a heat gun or by placing it close to a hot light bulb. Gradually and continually heating the full length of the sample will allow you to more than double its length. This demonstrates the great elongation capability of high performance cast vinyl. You should observe that the adhesive on good quality vinyl will also elongate yet remain intact; this is because of the adhesive's flow capability. Taken together, the flexibility of the vinyl and the adhesive allow you to conform high performance cast vinyl to compound curves and corrugated surfaces.

WARNING! Calendered vinyl does not perform as well or retain a stretched shape and should therefore not be used for curved and corrugated applications.

There is just one hitch to this experiment. As you stretch the vinyl, it becomes narrower. In fact, it will shrink to about 1/4-in. width. Doubling the sample's length reduces its width by half. When cutting vinyl, keep these proportions in mind and compensate for this dimensional reduction. Most simple or gentle curves can be worked with little or no addition of material; they may only require a quick trim along any edge distortion. For more extreme curves, the dimensions of the piece should be adjusted so that you have something to grab and stretch. Distortion and excess material can then be "erased" by trimming with your knife.

This technique works well for striping, but what about lettering or graphics? Occasionally, you'll need to add or piece-in material when the graphic distorts beyond your ability to re-shape it with a knife. Obviously, your graphics will be easier to re-shape if they are smaller along one axis or dimension; design with this in mind.

Designing your graphics to avoid curved or corrugated areas is an even easier way avoid facing application challenges. Or you can lay out the design — on a helmet for instance (the ultimate monster compound curve!) — with masking or fine line tape. Then apply a large piece of bulk, raw vinyl to the surface and use "pull" and heat to trim the design inside your guidelines.

The squeegee you select will affect your ability to contend with compound curves. A flat-bladed squeegee is not suitable for this type of application. Your thumb and fingers, however, work very well. A surface-conforming squeegee (remember the chopped off paint brush?) is also suitable, if you have a dense bristle pattern and firm contact. Working the application into the proper position on a compound curve can be a real challenge; you may have to press, pull, press, snap back past the point of contact, re-press, continue to pull, stretch and squeegee. And yet you'll still have to use your knife to remove edge distortions and re-shape!

Corrugated truck beds can stymie the most experienced applicator.

Fortunately, there is a growing trend toward smooth surface trailers. But meanwhile, when faced with this application situation . . . allow plenty of time. Corrugated surfaces require careful and proper squeegee use. The squeegee you use may be your thumb or fingers depending on the width, height, and frequency of the corrugations. If the trailer side looks like a panel of corrugated metal roofing, you will be doing a lot of finger squeegeeing!

Ribbed type trailers with raised spars — common on horse trailers — have flat panels separated by protruding ribs. Apply the graphic between the ribs if at all possible. If you must overlay one or more ribs, apply the graphic between the rips and up their sides. Bulk vinyl can be used to "cap" the ribs, and should then be trimmed to blend with your graphics. If you overlap the "cap" vinyl down the sides of the ribs, seams will be unnoticeable.

When working with any corrugated surface — even corrugated plastic yard signs — your squeegee blade should be parallel with the corrugations or flutes. Because flute seams are lower than the material face, squeegeeing across the flutes creates "valleys" of air; in-line squeegeeing prevents this bubbling. A surface-conforming squeegee works well for pressing the vinyl into such crevices. For effective squeegeeing, this orientation principle always applies: keep a squeegee parallel to the line of the corrugation, but move the brushes or fingers along the flutes to the edges of the graphic.

One final point: pre-converted vinyl striping products generally have a clear polyethylene mask which conforms better to curves and corrugations than a paper mask. Pre-converted vinyl striping also retains its original dimensions with less distortion prior to mask removal.

Be sure to orient your squeegee correctly when working on corrugated surfaces. Always keep the squeegee you're using parallel to the line. In contrast, move brushes (or your fingers) along the line from the center to the edges.

"Turning" striping involves stretching the material on the outside of the turn while pressing the inside of the turn so that wrinkles don't form. This is accomplished by pulling the stripe with one hand, and rubbing the stripe through the turn with the other (or with a squeegee). Remember: fingers are more sensitive than squeegees to the turning process.

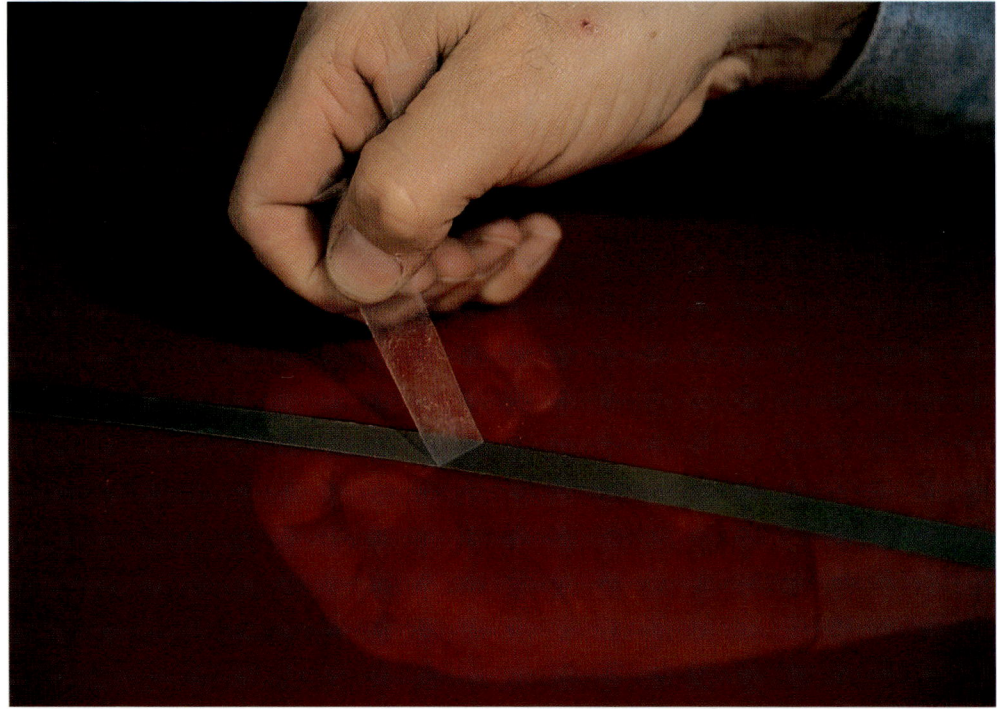

Remove any clear polyethylene mask. It has more "memory" than the vinyl and pulls the vinyl loose in the turns.

ADVANCED VINYL APPLICATION • 35

Always tighten the core before using a roll of striping. Hold the core and pull the stripe tight. It's a simple process that will save a lot of grief.

The proper way to hold striping and dispense it from a roll is to hold the roll and the core in one hand. Hold the release liner with two fingers from the same hand. When you start applying, use your free hand to guide the laying of the stripe.

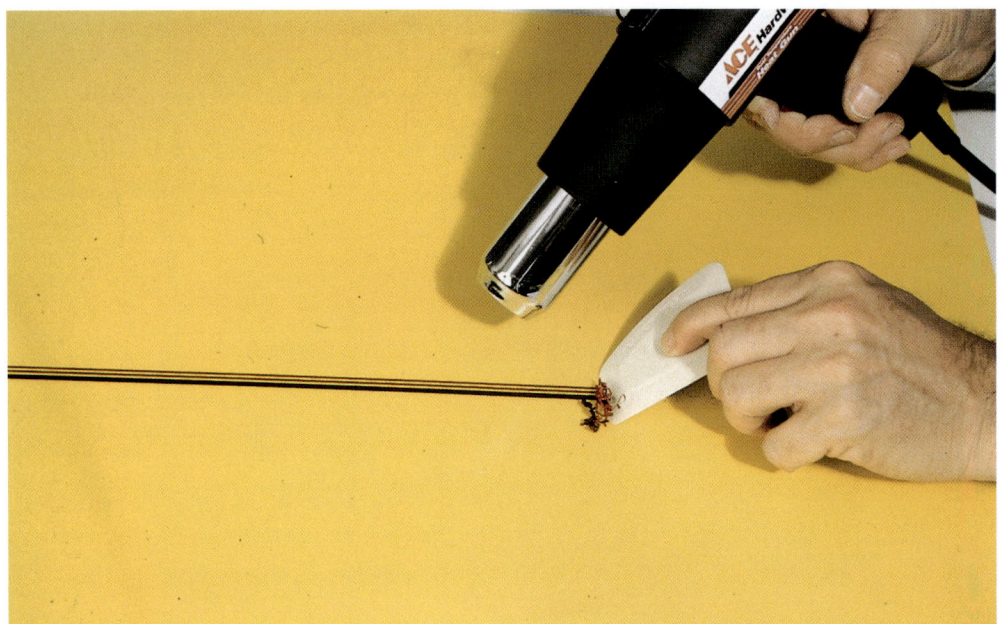

To remove vinyl that is old and fragmented, it is often necessary to employ a heat gun, heat lamp, or a gas torch. You may also need to scrape the vinyl with a tool like the "Li'l Chiseler."

If the vinyl film is still intact, lift the film, pulling it back at a 30° angle to the surface. Doing so causes the adhesive to shear off with the vinyl. Because rubbing and scraping the adhesive won't be necessary, much adhesive removal time will be saved.

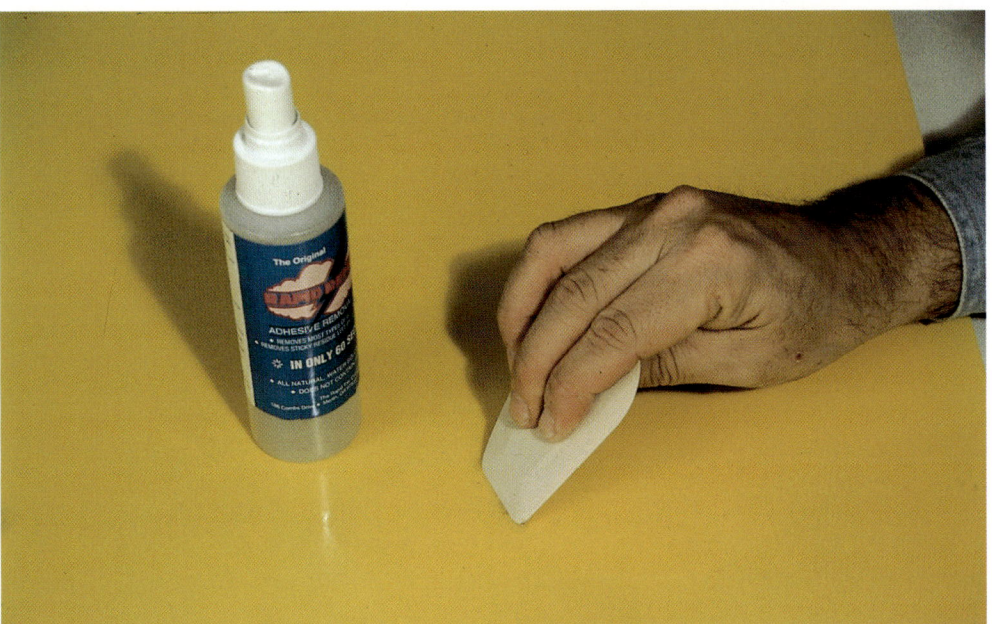

Sometimes it's necessary to remove vinyl with chemicals. Di-limonene or citrus-based adhesive removers are marketed as safer alternatives to petrochemical solvents.

Textured substrates

MASTER PRINCIPLE: *Conformation, not adhesion, is the key issue with textured surfaces. There is actually more surface area on a textured substrate than a flat one. You just have to get down to it.*

The acrylic adhesive system on a high performance, cast vinyl film is remarkable in its ability to latch onto and hold a variety of materials. I have had vinyl stick to the rubber sole of my shoe and not come off for months until I removed it. (The vinyl that is, not my shoe!) My wife has located lost graphics stuck on the bottom of the washing machine several months after I lost them. Years later . . . still there! I have seen and applied vinyl to stucco, brick and even roofing shingles, and the graphics have lasted for years. Adhesion is rarely the problem. Getting the vinyl adhesive into contact with the surface is the challenge.

Quite simply, the vinyl must assume the surface texture of the substrate. Apply heat to improve the vinyl's malleability . Then place the vinyl in contact with the textured surface by using a surface-conforming squeegee (a chopped paint brush). Work slowly until you get the hang of using a heat gun with a brush on a rough surface. Once the vinyl adheres, remove the mask gradually. If needed, apply more heat and continue to brush. Do not overheat to the point of curling the edge of the vinyl. Do hair dryers work? Yes . . . for drying your hair! But not for this! Invest in a good quality heat gun. Master Appliance™ and Dayton™ are well-known, industrial-quality heat gun suppliers. Paint stripper heat guns, readily available in hardware stores, work well and are no more expensive than good quality hair dryers. Just be sure you don't get confused and try to dry your hair with a heat gun!

When heated, vinyl becomes more malleable. Place the vinyl in contact with the textured surface by using a surface-conforming squeegee (chopped paint brush). Work slowly until you're comfortable using a heat gun with a brush on a rough surface.

Removal techniques

MASTER PRINCIPLE: *The health of the vinyl graphics industry relies on providing safe, fast, reasonably priced removal service. It can also be a very profitable.*

Removing vinyl requires heat or the use of very strong chemicals. Any chemical used to remove vinyl or adhesive must be properly used and disposed. Some chemicals have been proven hazardous, while other so-called "safe" chemicals have probably not been sufficiently tested to determine long-term health effects from their usage. It is therefore advisable to err on the side of caution. Obtain manufacturer safety recommendations for proper chemical usage.

In some instances (for example, truck trailers or outside walls), a combination of chemicals and high pressure sprayers is very effective. For these removal situations, apply the chemical with a garden sprayer, give it time to work, and blast with a high-pressure sprayer. Again, properly dispose of the waste from this procedure.

Certain "repositionable" film products like Controltac™ make removal easier down the road. But beware; there are many materials that do not have this ease-of-removal built into them. In fact, many are just the opposite. With these, you need to know how to quickly pull the vinyl and remove any adhesive residue without damaging the substrate.

Because of the aforementioned health considerations, I prefer to use heat instead of chemicals when removing vinyl. Often the sun's heat on a warm day is sufficient to facilitate removal. But if the vinyl is old and fragmented, a heat gun, heat lamp or gas torch should be employed. Again, be careful when working with sources of heat — especially open flames. Get the film very warm to the touch. You can then safely scrape the vinyl with a "Li'l Chiseler" — a pocket tool I call my "2-in. wide thumbnail."

Available from Film Handler Tools, this scraper is made from polycarbonate and does not scratch most surfaces.

If the film is still intact, lift the vinyl and pull it back at about a 30° angle to the surface. This method causes the adhesive to shear off with the vinyl and will save you much removal time. Further, it prevents surface marring caused by chemicals, towels and scrapers. A combination of two-parts MEK (methyl ethyl ketone) and one-part xylene makes a fast and effective chemical adhesive remover. Just be sure to exercise appropriate caution in its use. Di-limonene or citrus-based adhesive removers are marketed as safer alternatives to petrochemical solvents.

Rotary rubber erasers and self-destructive pads that mount to high-torque drills are sold for removing vinyl and adhesive. Used properly, they are safe and effective on most substrates. I've found, however, that they are slower than my heat gun/ correct pull angle/"Li'l Chiseler"/ chemical adhesive remover method.

It is quite likely that new chemical alternatives and easier-to-remove vinyls and adhesive systems will be invented. In the meantime, our industry must accept the responsibility to offer removal service to those who have purchased and enjoyed our vinyl graphics products in years past. We must also remove inferior applications at a reasonable cost, or if we originally installed the offending product, free-of-charge. Suitable removal tools and methods exist; we should practice skillfully using them.

MASTER PRINCIPLE: *Advanced performance and superior results are expected from "masters of the craft." Always remember that a master is — first and foremost — a student. Never stop learning new and better ways to master the craft.*

SPECIALIZED VINYL APPLICATION

This final chapter on vinyl discusses specialized application considerations: translucent and retro-reflective films; goldleaf films; painting, airbrushing and color imaging; and heat transfer graphics.

Translucent and retro-reflective films

Master principle: Adjust your handling of specialized films to compensate for their unique characteristics.

Circumstances sometimes dictate the use of specialized film. Your vinyl graphics may, for example, need to be visible at night. This desired visibility is obtained by either back-lighting the graphics or by front-lighting them with a source light.

In the first situation, use translucent films on back-lit clear or translucent substrates. Doing so assures the transmittal of uniform color, day or night. Opaque film can be combined with this type of production and used as block-out film — film that appears one color during the day, yet seems black at night. By using diffuser films such as Scotchcal™ Series 3635-30 or Series 3635-70, clear substrates can be made translucent. If you need maximum graphic protection for the face of the sign, you can use GPS (Scotchcal™ Series 3640-114 HA film), Rexcal 6000 2-mil cast, fluoropolymer film, or a 1-mil cast, fluoropolymer film available from SignGold Corp. 3M's excellent "Tips for Translucents" guide offers additional suggestions and information for this application situations, and can be obtained by calling (800) 328-3908.

Some fundamental translucent graphic tips include:

1. When a customer wants a matte finish, use first-surface application. The image and background color — if used — should be applied to the front side of the substrate (which is usually a diffuse white surface). The image should be cut to be right-reading.

2. For a glossy finish or added graphic protection, use second-surface application. The image and optional background color should be applied to the back side of a clear, rigid substrate. The images should be cut in reverse, and colors should be applied in the opposite order of first-surface applications.

3. Because polycarbonate substrates absorb moisture, they can outgas and form bubbles. Adding layers of film increases this bubbling potential. Follow the substrate manufacturer's recommendations for drying and sealing substrates prior to film application. Also, apply manufacturer-recommended sealants to both sides of polycarbonate substrates to prevent outgassing, panel warp and distortion.

4. Prep surface with water and tar, wax, grease, and silicone remover. Then, dry them before the solvent evaporates. Wiping with alcohol or dryer anti-static sheet helps discharge static pockets.

5. Use wet application methods when applying translucent films. As always, squeegee properly: Move from the center to the edges with firm, overlapping strokes.

6. Avoid seaming; try to use whole sections of film. If overlapping films is necessary, however, use a 1/32-in. overlap to minimize the seam and prevent potential leaks from weathering. Should two or more pieces of the same color film need to be seamed into a continuous band, use film from the same roll or lot. To assure a uniform appearance, "swing" matching edges to meet each other.

7. Put dark color films over light colors and overlap them 1/32-1/16 in. to compensate for registration errors. The darker overlap helps frame the lighter color.

8. Internal lamps may show on the face of the production as streaks, hot spots or bright outlines. Eliminate or reduce this undesirable effect by applying diffuser film to the back of the face. Deeper cabinets or multiple layers may be required as well.

Using light-reflecting film is another way to give graphics nighttime visibility. This film is more properly referred to as retro-reflective film since the film returns light to its source, rather than reflecting the light in the opposite direction. When applied to signs and vehicles, retro-reflective film does much more than provide around-the-clock visibility; it saves lives and prevents property damage.

Retro-reflective film's light-directing capability comes from either an intense accumulation of micro-fine glass beads or from an angular prism effect precisely etched onto its surface. To block translucency and to enhance color intensity and reflectivity, retro-reflective film usually has white or silver pigment added to its adhesive system. Because this construction makes the film heavy, it tends to sag; installing in smaller lengths (especially when striping) is advised. Heat should be avoided except when spot-softening around rivet heads. Also, it is better to install this film using dry application methods. Use good squeegee techniques and remove bubbles with the puncture-and-push method.

SPECIALIZED VINYL APPLICATION • 39

Reflective truck/trailer marking kits are available through 3M.

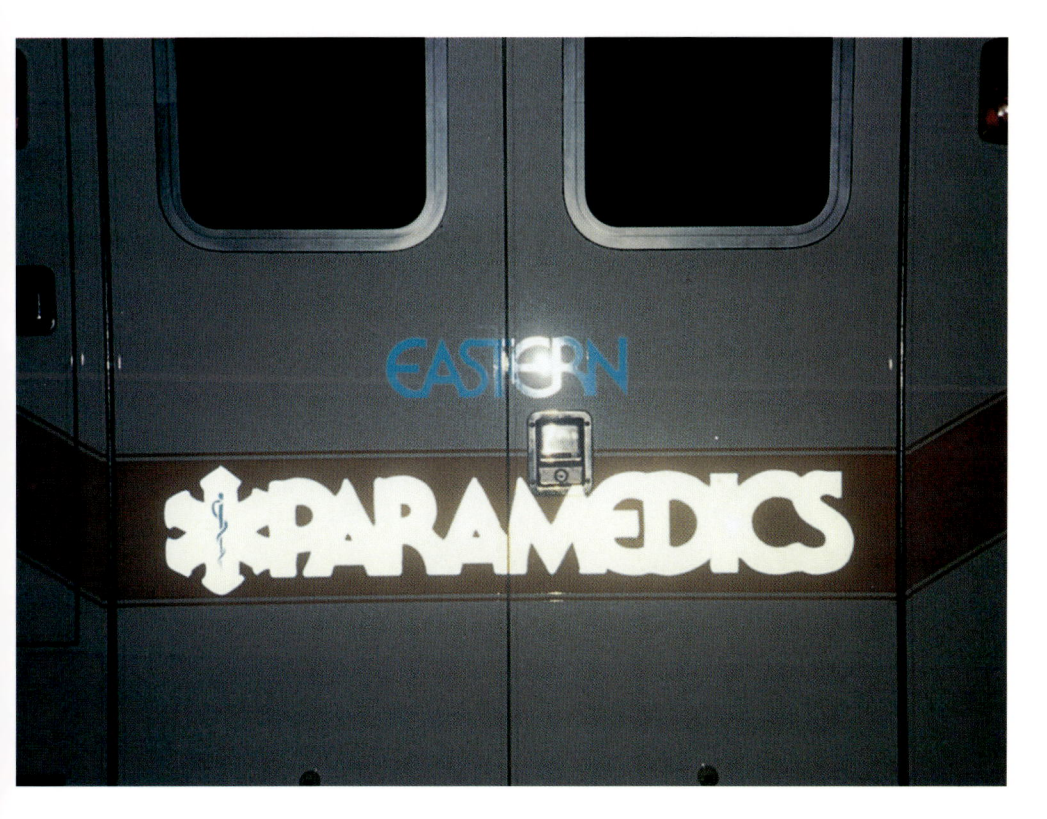

Graphics with nighttime visibility can save lives.

Genuine goldleaf film

Master principle: Goldleaf, whether hand- or pre-assembled, comprises an adhesive system, a layer of fine gold and a protective surface coating.

One of the most advanced or specialized signmaking methods is goldleaf. It can take many years of dedicated practice to achieve artistic results with goldleaf — results that look great and last many years.

By using a genuine gold, self-adhesive film, however, this learning curve can be significantly shortened, artistic results can be speedily produced, and the life of the finished production can be greatly enhanced. At the same time, maintenance procedures can be streamlined if the protective surface coating resists pollution and solvents. Fluoropolymer surface coatings make the film graffiti-proof and fade-resistant.

Films of this caliber are available in the marketplace and can easily be hand- or computer-cut. First-surface finishes such as matte, engine turn, and special grain patterns are offered, as are mirror- and matte-second-surface films. Pre-converted pinstriping is also available, and can be used to border signs or accent vehicles. Real gold requires no edge sealing and fluoropolymer coating requires no waxing. Ten- to 14-year acrylic adhesive systems allow you to offer your customers long warranty coverage for your productions.

The high-perceived value of real gold and silver, coupled with the convenience of speedy delivery, enable you to charge as much for these productions as for hand applied metal. Remember, it is poor marketing to diminish the value of your productions or those of other skilled craftspeople.

Applying the genuine gold, self-adhesive film pictured here is much easier to learn than hand-gilding. Another advantage to this type of film is the ease with which it can be cut, installed and maintained.

Paints, coatings and finishes

Master principle: *When adding color, shading or texture to vinyl, use durable, compatible paints, inks and clearcoats.*

Recent advances in paints, inks, and clearcoat products make it possible to create productions that incorporate mixed media. You can easily combine vinyl's durability and ease of production/application with the inexpensive special effect capabilities of paint and airbrushing. By using a plotter that both cuts and sprays, it is even possible to automate airbrush activity *(see photo at top left)*. More expensive automated painting systems also work well with vinyl.

Special effects are achieved with paint on vinyl by brushing, rolling, sponging, spattering, webbing, texturing, marbleizing, water bubbling, crumpling, stenciling, solvent washing, screening, pressing, stamping, rubbing, masking, and resisting. In fact, with the proper paint, any artistic, creative effect used by painters of fine art can likewise be used on vinyl. If you study these effects and refer to the book *Professional Painted Finishes* by Ina Brosseau Marx, Allen Marx and Robert Marx, (the principles of The Finishing School — see the chapter on "The Art of Graining" and their book is available from ST Publications), you will be able to achieve striking results.

So that the colors do not distort if the film has to stretch over a textured substrate, compound curve, or flexible substrate, the paint or ink you use needs to approximate vinyl's flexibility, durability and elongation capability. These requirements should help you select appropriate paints and inks. And remember: If long-term durability is required, your painted graphic should be clear-coated. Certain automotive urethanes — those that have catalysts mixed with them — are good options.

Recent advances in vinyl technology allow it to be airbrushed. Also, it is now possible to automate airbrush effects by using a plotter that both cuts and sprays.

Special effects can be achieved on vinyl by brushing, rolling, sponging, spattering, texturing, stamping, etc. Shown here is a webbing process that is also possible.

Paint on enamel-receptive, clear vinyl is easy to produce in the shop and install on-site.

Heat transfer graphics

Master principle: There are many ways to bring added value and variety to your vinyl graphic productions.

In addition to pressure-sensitive adhesive systems, there are also heat-sensitive systems you can use. These make it possible to apply graphics to diverse substrates, including shirts, hats, car seats and horse blankets. Such applications complement graphics created on signs and vehicles. Using heat transfers, you can personalize your customers' belongings, increasing their "pride-of-ownership value." Company logos can also be generated then heat-transferred to cloth surfaces. Similarly, sublimation printers can make photo-realistic transfers for wearables, mugs, and other promotional tools. These options will prove attractive for your customers; they can enhance their advertising efforts by hiring you to put their company's name in front of more viewers. You may also gain business by graphically "decorating" your customer's business possessions with his/her company's name and logo.

Heat transfers can be produced in four major materials: thermal wax transfers, electro-static ink transfers, hot-split plastisol, and heat transfer flock. The first two are generally produced on special sublimation printers or by producers using screen production. These transfers are usually multi-color and complex designs are possible. The last two are usually hand-, die-, or computer-generated and are for simpler, single color designs.

Multiple colors can still be achieved by registering additional single colors. An added advantage of heat transfer flock is that it looks and feels like cloth. All these media have been designed for long-term durability, even when laundered regularly.

The traditional application tool for heat transfers is a heat press. Different types of presses exist for various articles of clothing. A certain type of press, for example, is used for shirts and jackets, while a different press is used for hats. Still another type of press is used for cups with a specially prepared receptive surface.

Art-A-Tac™ is the first and only patent-pending, portable graphics application system for installing heat transfers *(see photo on next page)*. It enables easy, on-site application of graphics; the substrate need not be removed from its location and taken to an in-shop press. With this tool, for example, graphics can be applied to a vehicle's interior, without removing any upholstery cloth from the car. By coordinating exterior and interior graphics in this way, you become a truly full-service graphics installer. Subsequently, the value of your services is enhanced.

Mastery of craft

Master principle: Mastery is a path, not a destination. A master is, first and foremost, a student. Frustration inevitably occurs when a student hits a plateau; however, this is where most learning occurs. A true master perseveres through such plateaus and continues to climb.

By now you have come to understand that there are really no limits to what can be achieved with vinyl graphics. The only limits that exist are those you establish in your mind.

You have seen that vinyl can be combined in innumerable ways with other products, including paint, ink, goldleaf, heat transfers and dimensional signage. It can be installed on nearly any substrate, in nearly any environmental situation. If I had a good ship and a space suit, I would . . . .

Vinyl will literally go over rocks, under water and through dust. It is hindered only by those who do not educate themselves on its proper use or those who choose to use vinyl with inferior qualities. Remember, use the best, not the cheapest! Give your clients long-term value by offering excellent productions — not just cheap prices. Contribute to the strength of your industry by being the best you can be and by helping your competitor improve, too. Shake off pricing insecurity and use a published pricing authority like the *Official Sign Contractors' Pricing Guide* (available from ST Publications).

Finally, keep your eyes and ears tuned to your trade. Regularly participate in trade seminars and acquire all the educational tools you can find.

SPECIALIZED VINYL APPLICATION • 45

Vinyl makes a striking addition to dimensional wood signage.

Art-A-Tac™ is the first and only patent-pending graphics application system that makes on-site installation of heat transfer graphics possible.

VINYL GRAPHICS GALLERY

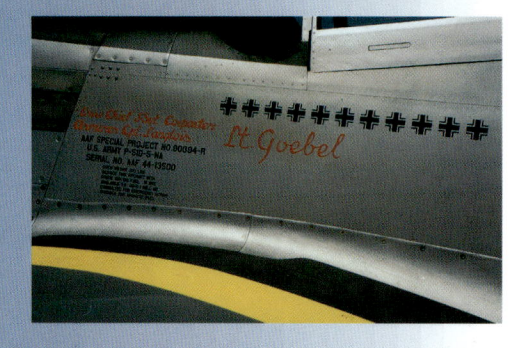

Larry Mitchell produced a series of vinyl stencils for precise painting in the restoration of this P-51 Mustang.

VINYL GRAPHICS GALLERY • 47

48 • SECTION ONE • VINYL

VINYL GRAPHICS GALLERY • 49

CONTENTS

6. Don Dozier, Making Banners — 53

7. Mark Goodridge, Screen Printing a Real Estate Sign — 60

Banners and Screen Printing

INTRODUCTION • *Don Dozier*

It boasts the highest profit margin of any sign company franchise in the industry. Of its 245 locations and 11 years in business, it has had only one business franchise failure for strictly financial reasons. It provides training, field support representatives, marketing and database support, site selection and lease negotiation, slick brochures, group purchasing discounts, operational bulletins and newsletters, a national accounts program, employee hiring guides, equipment and support, national and regional conventions—in short —a turnkey operation.

"It," is American Fastsigns, the fastest growing sign company in the world, with $74 million in sales, (about $350,000 per franchise) and projected sales approaching $200 million within the next five years.

American Fastsigns knows its niche, claims Don Dozier, the COO at the Dallas-based corporate headquarters, and that niche is not selling backlit signs or awnings, outdoor billboards, or custom crafted signs. Those types of projects are either subcontracted or passed on to others who specialize in the custom electric or commercial sign businesses. As its name suggests, American Fastsigns is in the quick sign business: banners, real estate signs, ADA work, restaurant signs, tradeshows and exhibit work, vehicle and corporate identification.

One-day signshops are a reality made possible thanks to developments in computer and vinyl technology. And a decade in business outperforming the rest of the sign industry has made other sign companies recognize the niche as legitimate. "Only four years ago," says Dozier, "there was a tremendous amount of resentment from the sign industry proper. We were looked at as a Johnnie-come-lately, not as a real sign company." However, above-industry average profit figures have spoken for themselves.

Dozier believes the quick sign business is recession resistant and can actually thrive when times are tough and businesses make greater use of one time sales and promotional banners to sell product. The quick sign business also has less of a need for skilled labor and capital equipment. Dozier knows this well from his experience at Federal Sign, the nationally-renowned electric sign company. Few can argue that one-day sign businesses show tremendous promise. American Fastsigns' growth is phenomenal: nearly 40 franchises per year are added. The international market, which the company deliberately waited to get into until its domestic side had a solid core, is now beginning to grow in Mexico, the UK and the Pacific rim.

Meanwhile, Dozier was recently recognized by the International Sign Association (formerly NESA) as one of the 20 industry experts to help formulate the association's mission statement. "I think we began to build credibility about four years ago," he says. "I was actually asked to come to the association convention and provide workshops. We did that for two consecutive years."

Recognition of success has come from outside the sign industry as well. *Success* magazine rated American Fastsigns in 1993 as the number one business-to-business franchise opportunity in the US. *Inc.* magazine has also had kind words for the training program they offer. But no kinder words have come from the owners of the franchises themselves, who are profiting well from their investments in American Fastsigns.

Don Dozier
American Fast Signs

MAKING BANNERS • 55

The excess vinyl is stripped away from the backing paper (weeded), leaving the design in place.

The design elements are carefully positioned and applied to the sign surface.

The finished sign.

Materials Chart

	Vinyl Receptive	Range of Colors	Outdoor Durability	Approx. Range of Weights
Vinyl	Yes	High	Long Term	8-18 oz
Polyethylene	Yes	Low	Short Term	8 oz
Nylon	Somewhat	High	None	4-18 oz
Canvas	No	Low	Long Term	8-18 oz
Tyvek	Yes	Low	None	4 oz
Cloth	No	High	None	4-6 oz

MAKING BANNERS • 57

Two examples of all-vinyl banners. Above, is a 3 x 6-ft. light-pole banner, and at right is a wall-mounted banner.

These are examples of screen-printed banners.

INTRODUCTION • Mark Goodridge

A successful screen printer in his own right who has been awarded a string of printing excellence awards, and more recently the editor of a national textile printing magazine, can laugh about it now. In 1982, when Mark Goodridge began his career, it might not have seemed so funny that his first job, screen printing a sign, cost $250 in materials, but it only paid $15. For his next job he printed $43 of placemats for his mother—and so Goodridges Screen Printing Services, a mom and pop shop Goodridge ran with his wife in Maine, was off and running.

For those first two years, Goodridge claims he specialized in losing money. But along the way, he also began to gain a reputation for high quality poster printing. Indeed, his work became well enough respected for him to almost annually receive awards for Printing Excellence from the Maine Graphic Arts Association.

Quality work generally results in business growth. By 1984, he had landed some major shopping mall accounts through ad agency clients and had begun to extend his sales to customers outside of Maine. His work became well known enough that his client base—primarily ad agencies—spread from Maine all the way down the coast to Florida. During that time, his business sense apparently improved. Within a few years, he was peaking at a quarter million dollars in gross sales and six employees.

Goodridge also gained a national reputation as a technical writer on screen printing and related topics. His articles have been published in trade magazines in the US and Europe and in the Technical Guidebook Series published by the Screenprinting and Graphic Imaging Association (formerly SPAI). Goodridge is also the author of the well-respected booklet, *Pricing for Profits,* an estimating and pricing guide for textile screen printers.

In 1992, a decade after he began his business, Goodridge was hired to be the editor of the national garment printing magazine, *Screenplay.* Goodridge has relocated from Maine (where he loved all four seasons) to Cincinnati, a city he claims has four seasons, all of which happen to be bad. Weather notwithstanding, fair winds have been blowing for Goodridge, who now can combine his screen printing expertise with a terse, no-nonsense writing talent. For more information on screen printing of all kinds, from signs to T-shirts, contact ST Publications, which publishes the monthly trade journals *Screen Printing* and *Screen Printing en español*, and several books on the subject.

Mark Goodridge
Technical Advisor for Screen Printing

Today, signpainting and screen printing are considered two different crafts, but this was not always the case. Signpainters in New York and Chicago developed the technology that became what we now know as screen printing. I ran a screen printing business for many years and I screen printed numerous signs for my own customers and for local signpainters.

Screen printing may seem daunting at first, especially in the middle of the first-printing run, when the inexperienced screen printer drops the squeegee, splashes ink on several completed signs and pokes a hole in the screen just as the phone rings. However, screen printing is really a fairly simple process that can produce an attractive, profitable product with a modest investment of time and money. If you can cook, you can screen print. Like cooking, your screen printing will improve with practice, but your first experiments are likely to be embarrassing if you don't follow instructions carefully.

Screen printing vocabulary

Before I get started, I want to explain some screen printing vocabulary. The process we're going to use is called screen printing, not silk screening or silk screen printing. Using the word "silk" in this context immediately identifies you as a complete novice or someone whose training and experience are 30 years out of date.

The mixture of pigments, binders, viscosity modifiers, solvents and other chemicals that we will use to decorate the sign blank is called "ink" — not "paint" — even when we run out on Saturday morning and buy an emergency gallon at the local Sherwin-Williams store.

The screen consists of a frame of wood or metal, stretched with mesh made of polyester fibers (this is what happens to bad leisure suits when they die). The mesh count is simply the number of threads per linear inch that are woven into the mesh.

In addition to the ink and screen, the one other indispensable tool of the modern, high-tech screen printer is the squeegee. (Don't blame me, I didn't name it.) Squeegees are available with wood or metal handles. Save money by buying wood. The squeegee blade is a thick, rubbery piece of plastic; do not economize on the blade. Get the best the supplier has to offer; generally, a proprietary variation of polyurethane. Good squeegee blades print better and last longer. Squeegee blades come in various hardnesses. Ask for a medium hardness. (By the way, the longer the squeegee, the more difficult it is to print with, so it's a good idea to always print with the squeegee running parallel to the shortest dimension of the sign. However, the squeegee should be at least 2 in. longer than the widest design you plan to print.) The real-estate signs we're going to print are 18 x 24 in. We'll print with the squeegee running parallel to the 18-in. dimension, so we'll need a squeegee 20 in. long.

The tools of the trade

In addition to screens, inks and squeegees, you will need the following tools and supplies:
- A screen printing "jig" consisting of a printing surface (a smooth table top or sheet of plywood will do) with hinge clamps attached (see photo 1)
- A box full of shop rags to clean up the mess afterwards
- Practice blanks (Sheets of paper or cardboard that you can practice printing on before you start printing on your expensive sign blanks)
- Ink stirrers
- Clean ink-mixing cans
- Plastic gloves
- A plastic or heavy cloth apron
- A kick leg — a wood slat that attaches to the frame of the screen to hold it off the surface of the printing jig when you're between prints (see photo 8)
- Lots of old newspapers
- Several pieces of 5 x 8-in. cardboard

In addition to the ink, you should order one quart each of two ink modifiers: reducer — to adjust the viscosity of the ink; and retarder — to slow the drying of the ink in case this happens in the screen. Also purchase a gallon of screen wash to clean the screens and squeegees after printing. Various types of ink require different reducers, retarders and screen washes. The supplier who sells you the ink will also sell you the appropriate products in these categories.

You will need a drying rack — a wooden jig or fixture to place the freshly printed signs on while they dry. (Laying freshly printed signs out on the lawn behind the shop invariable results in grasshoppers stuck in the wet ink and sudden, unpredicted rain squalls.)

You can make a simple, cheap drying rack by cutting a series of saw kerfs slightly wider than the thickness of the sign blanks, about 1 in. apart and 3/4-in. deep across the (nominal) 4-in. dimension of a 2 x 4-in. board. Lay this board on the floor with the saw kerfs up, where it will be out of traffic and away from dust, and you can slide the edges of the printed signs into the saw kerfs to hold so they can dry.

You will also need a helper. Although an experienced screen printer can easily print an order of real-estate signs alone, this does not apply to your situation. Until you gain screen-printing experience, two hands and two feet just aren't enough. Your helper should hand you the unprinted blanks, take away and rack the printed signs, answer the phone and be prepared to wipe ink off the squeegee handle, your hands and the toilet seat.

SCREEN PRINTING A REAL ESTATE SIGN

The sign blank

Your first decision involves the substrate you'll use. Whichever type you select, I strongly suggest that you purchase blanks that are cut to size and pre-coated. You may be strongly tempted to save money by buying large sheets and cutting and priming them yourself. Don't do it. This is more work than it's worth.

Real-estate sign blanks must be rugged, cheap, durable and very printable. Although real-estate signs are occasionally printed on heavy, weatherproof poster board, the more commonly used materials include: corrugated plastic, which is good for 1-3 years of continuous exterior exposure; hardboard; expanded-sheet PVC; and coated sheetmetal. All of these materials should be good for at least three years of continuous exterior exposure anywhere in North America. The determining factor will be which material your customers prefer, and how much they are willing to pay.

Ink selection

Once you determine your sign-blank material, you can — with some advice from your screen printing supplier — select an ink. Although special inks are formulated for each of the blank materials previously mentioned, in most cases, a good-quality, high-gloss, exterior-grade enamel will work well.

This type of ink is relatively inexpensive, widely available, weather- and fade-resistant, adheres well to most surfaces, looks good and is very easy to print with and clean up. The two materials that are exceptions are expanded PVC and corrugated plastic. Enamel will work on the PVC, but vinyl lacquers are better. If you intend to print on corrugated plastic, ask your screen printing supplier to recommend an ink specifically designed for that product.

Avoid Day-Glo or fluorescent colors. Under the best circumstances, these colors will show significant fading in 60-90 days. Use them only if the customer insists, and warn the customers about the fading.

Designing the sign

Usually, real-estate agencies will bring an old sign in for you to copy, but if you're starting with blank paper, here are some guidelines for designing real-estate signs.

Real-estate signs are printed on both sides in one or two colors, rarely more. Make the design bold and easy to read from a passing car. The primary copy should be the name of the agency. The secondary copy should be the agency's phone number. The easiest designs to print have white backgrounds, a good margin between the printing and the edge of the sign blank and don't require tight registration between the colors. You can draw the sign full size in black and white (one drawing for each color), cut the design from red masking film, or create it on a computer and print the design out on a laser printer.

Buying the screen

At this stage in your screen printing education, I suggest that you don't make your own screens. Most screen-printing suppliers offer finished screens with the design already imaged on the mesh, ready to print. When you order the screen, specify the inside dimensions of the frame, the mesh type and mesh count, and explain how you will provide the design to be printed to the screen maker.

Novice screen printers often make big mistakes by ordering their screens too small. Smaller screens are less expensive, but they are devilishly hard to use. Here's a rule of thumb for screen size: The margin between each side of the design and the inside of the frame should be at least 1/3 of the image size. Therefore, because we will print 18 x 24-in. signs, the inside dimension of the screen should be 30 x 40-in.

I reasoned:
1/3 of 18 = 6, so the top and bottom margins must be 6 in. each; 1/3 of 24 = 8, so the left and right margins must be 8 in. each; 18 + 6 + 6 = 30; and 24 + 8 + 8 = 40. This is the minimum size.

The mesh type should be monofilament polyester, and the mesh count is determined by the type of ink you will be printing. After selecting the sign blanks, ask your screen printing supplier to suggest a type of ink. Then ask for recommendations as to proper mesh count. If the supplier recommends a range of mesh counts, select one at the lower end. Lower mesh counts are stronger and easier to print with. If all else fails, request a screen with a mesh count ranging from 150-195. These mesh counts will work with almost any ink for printing real-estate signs.

Setting up the printing jig

After you've assembled all the supplies, sign blanks, ink and screens, you're ready to set up a printing jig and practice. Bolt the hinge clamps to a large table top or piece of plywood, clamp the screen in preparation for the color that prints first in the hinge clamps, and then slide one of the sign blanks under the screen.

Be sure to position the sign blank so that, when the screen comes down, the image area is correctly positioned over the blank. Swing the screen up, then carefully mark the location of the bottom and one edge of the positioned sign blank. Tape or staple three registration stops (small rectangles of poster board or plastic about 1 x 2 in. [see photos 5, 6 and 7]) to the surface of the printing jig so that one of the stops is at each end of the bottom of the sign, and one stop touches the side (about an inch from the bottom). The registration stops will ensure that you place every sign blank on the printing jig in the exact same position relative to the image on the screen.

Next, you must adjust the off-contact distance (see photos 9 and 10). This is the distance between the bottom of the screen and the top of the sign blank when both are positioned for printing. Place a sign blank on the registration stops and lower the screen all the way down. You must have a distance of 1/8- 1/4 in. between the screen mesh and the top of the sign blank.

You can adjust the screen up by taping spacers (washers or small thin scraps of wood) on the surface of the printing jig where they will hold up the corners of the screen that aren't clamped into the hinge clamps. The printing surface should be flat, and the off-contact distance even, across the entire surface of the sign blank. You may have to place shims between the bottom of the frame and the bottom jaws of the hinge clamps (see photo 11). If this adjustment is necessary, be careful not to move the screen out of register. You can also use short, round-headed wood screws in the corners of the frame to adjust the off contact.

1. The basic screen-printing setup. A screen-printing jig consisting of a flat printing surface with hinge clamps attached, the screens, ink, a squeegee and lots of rags.

2. Check the image on the screen against a copy of the design to ensure that the screen is correct.

3. Hinge clamps are used to attach the screen to the printing jig. Loose pin hinges can also be used, but they are less convenient.

4. *The easiest way to register the sign blank in the jig is to tape a full-size copy of the design in position on a sign blank. Center the artwork on the sign blank before you line up the sign blank under the screen.*

5. *The small orange rectangles at the bottom of the blank are registration stops.*

6. *Attach the registration stops to the printing surface with masking tape.*

7. The sign blank is properly positioned on the registration stops.

8. The kick leg holds the screen off the printing surface making it easier to position unprinted blanks and remove the printed signs.

9. Check the off-contact distance by pushing down on the screen.

Attaching a kick leg

The last step in setting up the printing jig is the attachment of the kick leg. Cut a light wood slat 2-3 ft. long (see photo 8). Drill a small hole through the slat about 3 in. from the end. Drill another hole about 1 in. into the edge of the bottom of the frame (about 1 ft. from the end of the frame away from the hinge clamps).

Carefully drive a small screw through the wood slat and into the frame. (This is no place to get careless. You don't want to damage the frame or tear the mesh at this point.) The wood slat should pivot on the screw. This slat is the kick leg. When it's turned with the long end down, it will hold the frame off the surface of the printing jig so that you can place and remove sign blanks. When it's pivoted so that it is parallel to and flat against the edge of the frame, it allows you to lower the screen into the printing position.

You can purchase ready-made metal kick legs with springs, that will lift the screen semi-automatically, and clamps, that will attach them to any screen from your screen printing supplier.

Once the screen, registration stops and kick leg are in place, you are ready for the ink. Open the can and stir the ink. Most screen printing inks are ready for use right from the can. The ink should have a viscosity somewhere between honey and heavy cream. It definitely should not be watery.

If the ink seems too thick, pour the amount needed to print the job into a clean can and add a small amount of reducer. Your screen printing supplier will provide you with data sheets for all the ink and ink modifiers they sell you if you ask, and these documents will have specific instructions for modifying your ink. Generally, for most inks, you can add up to 10% reducer without ill effects. (Remember, you can always add more, but you can never remove what you've already added.)

Add small amounts and stir the ink thoroughly every time. If the ink dries in the screen, add a small amount of retarder. Instructions for using retarder are also available from your supplier.

Once the ink is adjusted to your satisfaction, you're ready to start printing. But before you begin, make one last check. Do you have all the supplies and equipment on hand that you will need to complete the job? Screen printing is like ski jumping. Once you start, there's no convenient stopping place until the end. If this is your first time, you might want to unplug your phone, or at least turn on your answering machine.

Place a practice blank in the registration stops, lower the screen and then pour about a cup of ink onto the screen between the image area and the side of the frame held in the hinge clamps. Spread the ink a little toward the top and bottom of the frame and then make one print stroke across the image area of the screen. Do this by holding the squeegee in both hands, placing it in the ink pool, tip the squeegee handle about 15° out of vertical in the direction of the print stroke, push the squeegee firmly down and pull the squeegee toward you.

10. Adjust the off-contact distance by sliding a spacer under the corner of the frame.

11. The off-contact spacers can be attached to the printing surface with tape.

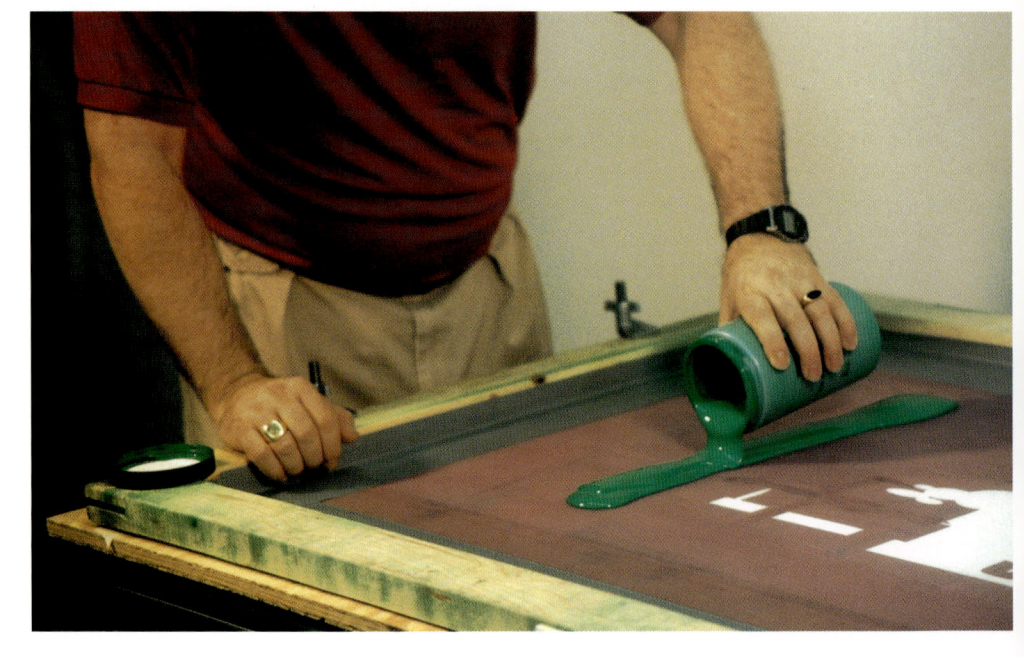

12. Don't flood the screen with ink. You can always add more during the print run.

13. Pull the squeegee toward you smoothly, slowly and with firm downward pressure.

Here are some tips. You don't have to move all the ink with every print stroke. Only pull enough ink to print the full image. You don't need to cover the entire surface of the screen with ink. In fact, a neat professional screen printer will only place ink on the screen where it is needed for printing. Try to avoid getting ink on the frame and the squeegee handle, at all costs. You should push down on the squeegee just firmly enough to bend the blade, but only slightly.

After the print stroke, you must make a "flood" stroke (see photo 14). Lift the screen a couple of inches and make a stroke in the direction opposite the print stroke with the squeegee blade held just a fraction of an inch above the screen. The purpose of the flood stroke is to cover the image area of the screen with a thin layer of ink without pushing the ink through the mesh. Don't worry, the ink won't drip through the screen on its own, or if it does, you thinned it down too much.

The layer of ink flooded over the image area of the screen by the flood stroke prevents ink from drying in the image areas of the screen and blocking the print. Practice printing and flooding until you are confident you can print a sign blank quickly and easily and obtain a sharp, even print. You're now ready to start printing the signs.

Your sign blanks should be wiped free of dust and stacked where they are near the printing jig, but not in the way or where likely to splash on them. You should have 3-5 extra blanks on hand over to allow for misprints. Check your hands for ink smudges. You don't want to leave your thumbprints all over the nicely printed signs. Print the first color on one side of each of the blanks (see photo 17) and stack each one neatly in the drying rack.

If you have any smears, smudged prints or misprints, you can clean up the print, or remove the entire print with screen wash. Lay the misprinted blank on a clean table with several layers of old newspapers underneath. Then, working quickly and making as little mess as possible, wipe clean the blank and then wipe it as dry as possible. Set the cleaned blank aside and print it last.

14. When you're making the flood stroke, lift the screen slightly with one hand.

After all the sign blanks have one color printed on the first side, you must clean the screen. Don't remove the screen from the printing jig. Place several layers of old newspapers under the screen. Put on plastic gloves and scrape as much of the ink out of the screen with the pieces of cardboard.

Put the excess ink back into the mixing can. Next, dampen a rag with screen wash and wipe as much ink as you can off the screen. Keep wiping the screen on both sides with fresh rags until you have removed as much of the ink as possible. When you've done this, take a break. You deserve it.

Before you start the next printing cycle, you must let the ink you just printed dry thoroughly. I used to print real-estate signs at the end of the day, timing my work so that I finished cleaning the screen at quitting time. This gave the printed blanks the entire night to dry. Once the print is thoroughly dry on the first side, print the same design on the second side. Then change screens, repeat the set-up procedure and print the second color on both sides just as you did the first.

Here are some general tips if you're new to screen printing.

Screen-printing is a messy process. Make an extra effort to keep you, your tools and your shop clean. If you don't, you'll find the ink in numerous unlikely and unwanted places (see photo 19).

The screen printing process will seem awkward at first. Overcome it by practice printing before you start putting ink on your good sign blanks.

Learn to be patient and work at a steady pace: not too fast and not too slow. You won't gain anything by hurrying.

Adjust your work schedule so that you can print each stage of the job without distractions or interruptions. Good luck.

15. Practice printing on large sheets of stiff paper until you're confident you can pull a good print on a sign blank.

16. Place the sign blanks on the register stops carefully and consistently.

SCREEN PRINTING A REAL ESTATE SIGN • 67

17. There's the first color print on a sign blank. Check carefully for correct placement of the image on the blank.

18. Once you've printed all the blanks with the first color on one side, remove the unused ink from the screen and the squeegee with rectangles of cardboard.

68 • SECTION TWO • BANNERS AND SCREEN PRINTING

20. Set up to print the second color the same way you set up for the first.

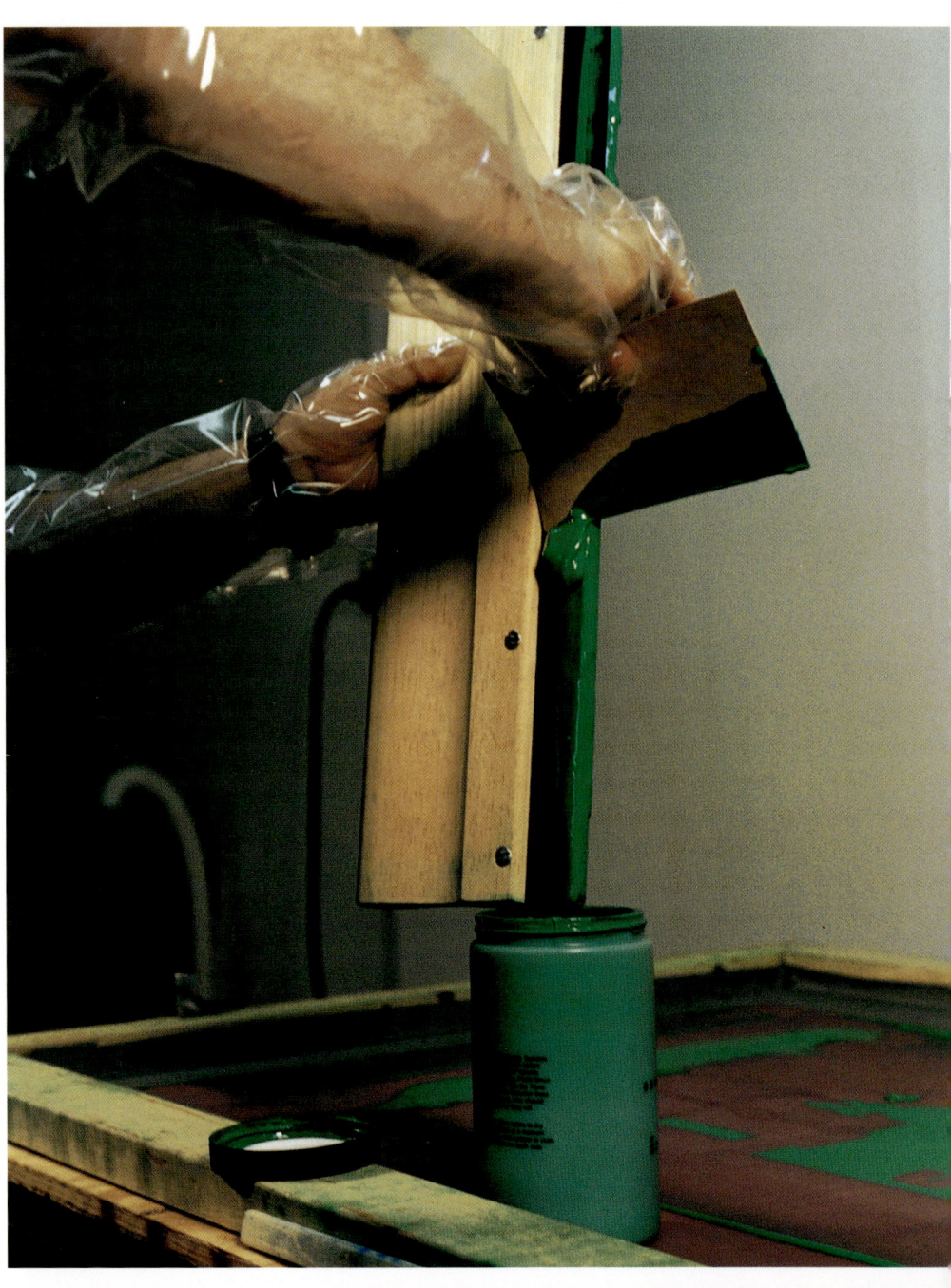

19. Wear plastic gloves to keep your hands clean.

21. *Voilá! The completed real-estate sign, colorful, durable and inexpensive. A simple job if you plan ahead and practice.*

CONTENTS

8. Nancy Beaudette and Noella Cotnam, Making a Multi-Dimensional Wood Sign   **74**

9. James Mitchell, Making a Blacksmith's Sign   **88**

SECTION THREE • *Wood*

MAKING A MULTI-DIMENSIONAL WOOD SIGN

This project was designed to be the finishing touch to our new wood shop and art studio in the country. The name Heron Cross was chosen because of the Great Blue Herons that nest in the river across the road from us.

Nancy sketched out the lettering and sign design at home one night, and programmed it on our computer at work. From there, we generated a scaled-paper pattern used to transfer the design to the redwood panel and to the sandblast stencil. We then drew the pattern in transfer ink in reverse using 100% Windex (sprayed on the stencil and paper to aid pattern transfer; as opposed to lacquer thinner which is commonly used) and a rubber brayer. Although the pattern can only be used once, the process is much healthier than using lacquer thinner or other strong solutions. (Note: We used high-density urethane manufactured by both Sign Art and Coastal Enterprises, so the letters may vary in color as we go through our carving steps.)

We use high-density urethane to add dimension to signs either through raised lettering, raised graphics or pictorials. We have found that high-density urethane is very consistent to carve and easy to work with. The biggest drawback of the product is that it becomes highly charged with static. It is vital that you wear a dust mask when sanding. At the end of the day, the dust will be stuck to every exposed part of your body. We believe it's a small price to pay for the end result, which is a beautiful dimension.

The pattern is transferred to the panel, the stencil is cut and the sign is sandblasted. We blast at 100 psi with 24-grit sand. The blast is at least 1/2 in. deep, and the halo blast around the main silhouette is approximately 1/4 in. deep.

Cotnam routs a 3/8-in. cove around the outside edge of the sign and then primes the sign with acrylic-latex primer. We apply one or two coats, depending on how well the first coat covers.

MAKING A MULTI-DIMENSIONAL WOOD SIGN • 75

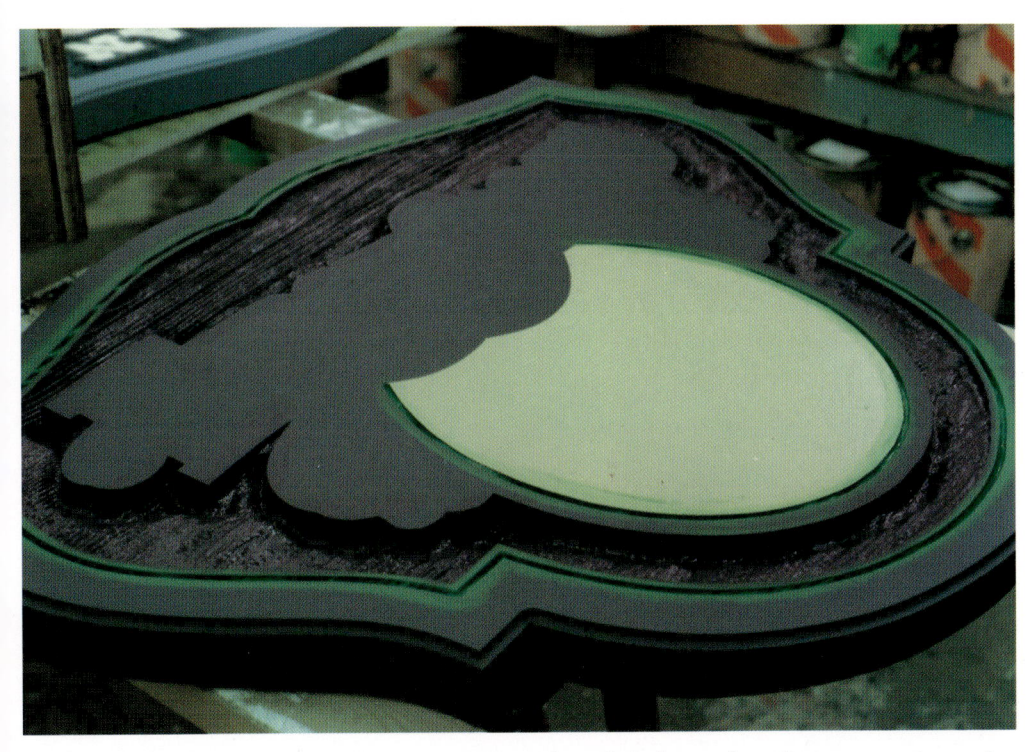

The sign is top coated with acrylic latex. We apply a rich purple background, medium-green stripes and a very dark purple border and silhouette. The pictorial area is then painted with straight ivory enamel.

The 1-in.-thick material is routed with a 1/8-in. drill bit. Before using the router, we cut our letters on a band saw. The smaller letters are 2-1/2 in. tall and the "H" is 5 in. high.

Gouges are required for carving high-density urethane prismatic letters. For the next part of the project, Cotnam uses a 1-in. Number 3 gouge and 1/2-in. and 1/4-in. Number 5 gouges. Cotnam also uses a rasp and various grits of sandpaper (mostly 120). Gouges are used to create an interesting concave shape in the top of the bevel.

This is the most critical part of the whole process: marking the guide lines. The line around the sides of the letter will help control the depth of the carving, and the line of top marks — the center guide — will help to control the angle of your chisel. (Note: Use two-way tape to hold the letters in place while they are being carved.)

These letters are carved somewhere between 25 and 30 in. Carving foam can dull your chisel very quickly, so buffing the chisel between letters is important. The sharper your tool, the more success you will have. Start to slice around the outside edges of the letter, taking off a bit at a time until you've connected your guide lines. With practice, you should be able to cut your bevels in one or two passes.

MAKING A MULTI-DIMENSIONAL WOOD SIGN • 77

The letter is stationary, so you have to change positions as you work.

Some positions may seem awkward at first, but they will become comfortable with practice.

When you carve the thinner portions of the letters, your cut becomes more shallow. This will happen automatically if you follow your guide lines. The beauty of urethane foam is that it maintains the same consistency regardless of which way it is carved. And, because there is no grain to contend with, your chisel moves through the substrate easily in any direction.

Perhaps the trickiest part of carving a fancy letter is understanding how the strokes will connect to each other. With this copy, we have let the horizontal "swish" connect to the vertical strokes naturally. If you maintain proper depth and angle, the intersections between horizontal and vertical strokes will happen on their own. (Note: Treat the tops and bottoms of the letters the same as the sides — follow the guide lines!)

Once the letters have been carved, use sandpaper to smooth out the chisel marks. (If you want a more "natural" look, you may leave the chisel marks. It all depends on the look you're trying to achieve.)

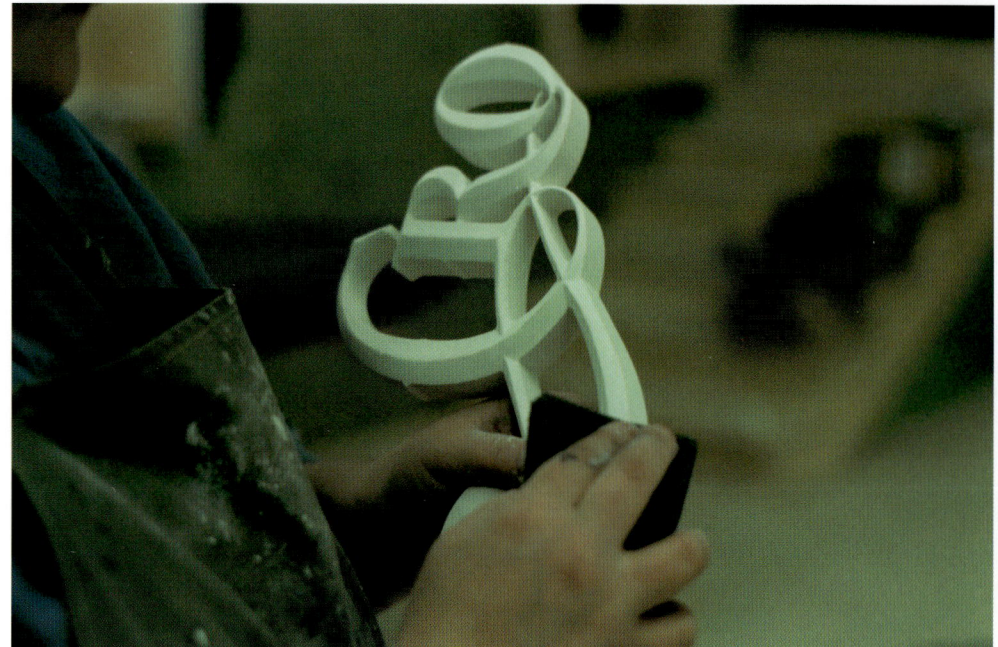

High-density urethane tends to be very porous and comes in various densities (the higher the number, the more dense the material). For this project, we chose 18-lb. foam.

As with any substrate, proper priming is imperative. For this project we use a high-build, water-based primer. Three coats are applied with a light sanding between each coat.

(Note: If you need to apply paste to fix a nick in the letter, be sure to do this after the first priming. If it is pasted before priming, it will stand out like a sore, glossy thumb ruining the final look.)

The letters are then given two top coats with a very lightly mixed ivory bulletin enamel. The scrolls are a light "dirty orangish color," which is accomplished by mixing a bit of purple and green to tan and orange.

MAKING A MULTI-DIMENSIONAL WOOD SIGN • 79

At Sign It, we work on the letters and the panel at an equal pace so that all components will be ready to put together at the same time. The heron is painted with lettering enamels and Cotnam uses Jones blending cream and Edge thinner as extenders.

We add another layer of dimension using 1/4-in. foamed PVC. It is painted high-gloss medium green, then siliconed and tacked down to the panel.

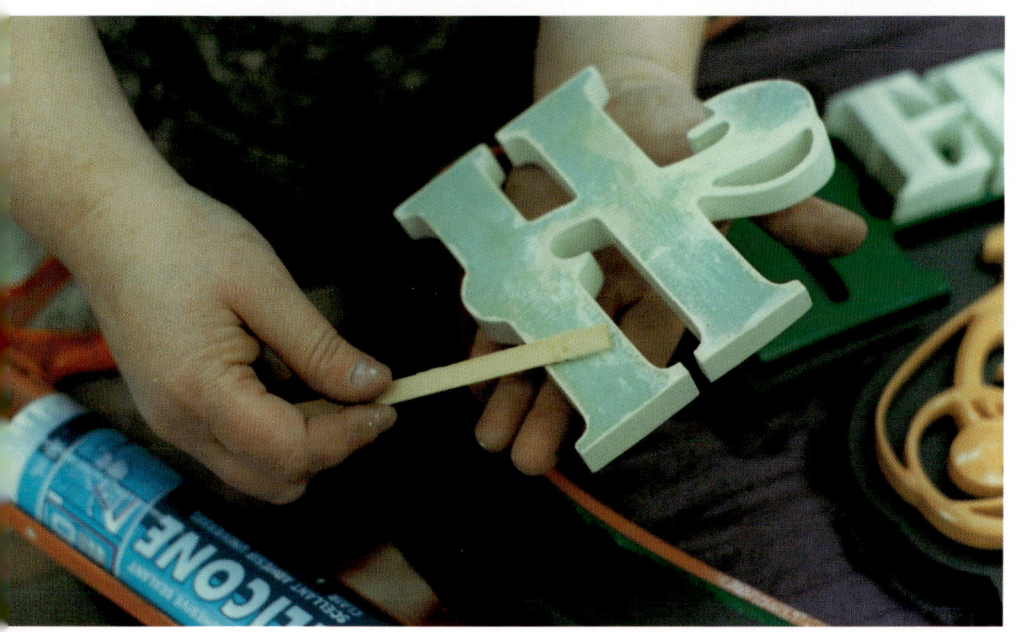

The letters and scrolls are secured to the sign by using silicone.

A darker (than what was used on the scrolls), "dirty orangish color" is used on the accent stripes.

A detail shot illustrating the many dimensions of the sign.

MAKING A MULTI-DIMENSIONAL WOOD SIGN • 81

Voilà! The finished sign is temporarily installed in front of our shop. The siding will be stained, and we intend to fabricate a bracket and hang the sign off the side of the building.

SIGN IT GALLERY

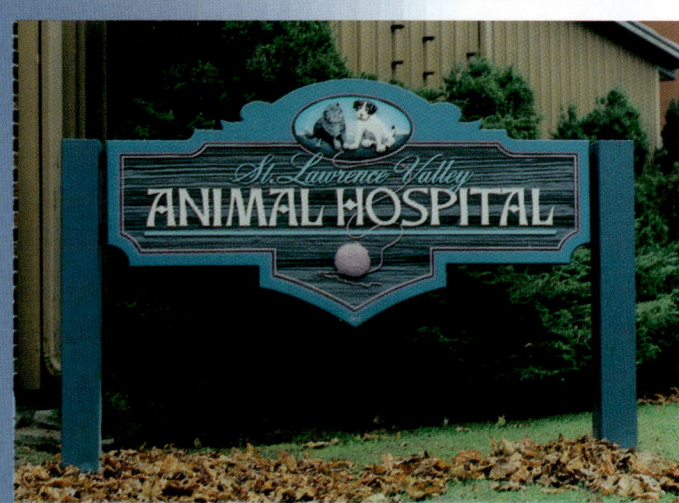

SIGN IT GALLERY • 83

84 • SECTION THREE • WOOD

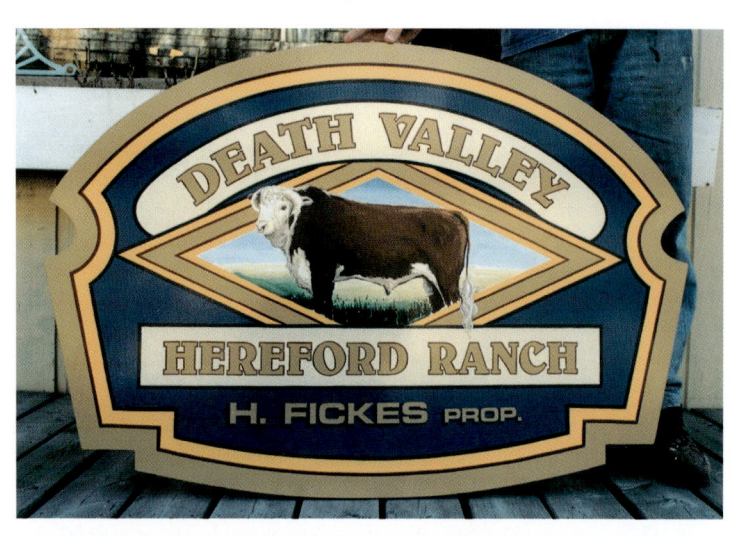

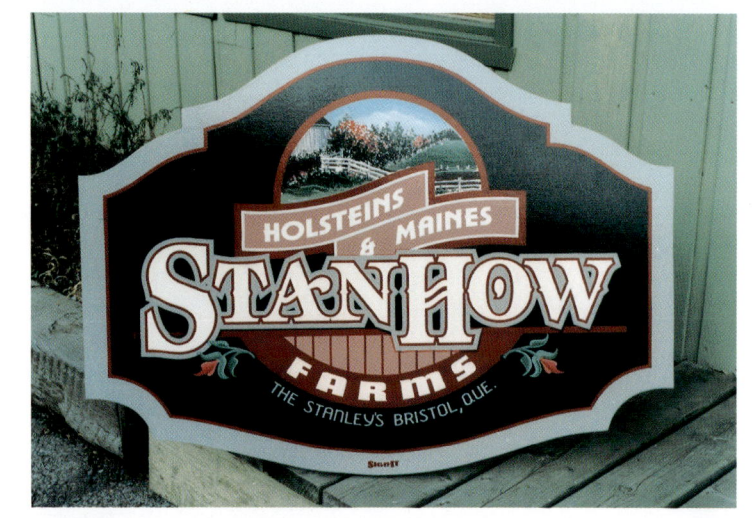

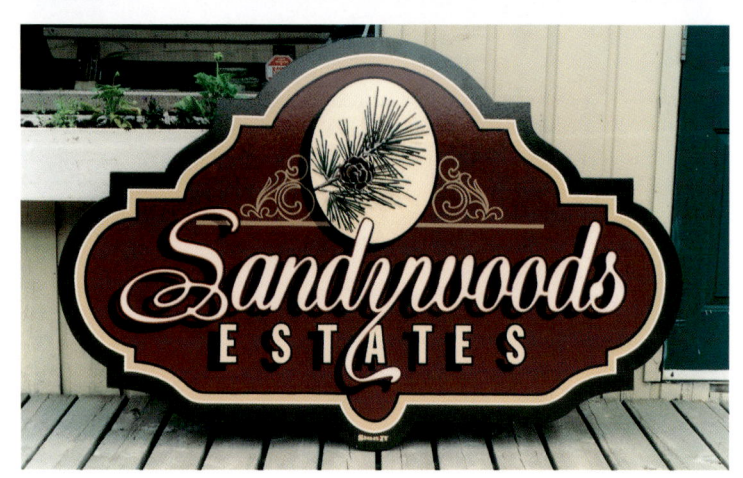

SIGN IT GALLERY • 85

INTRODUCTION • *James Mitchell*

In business since 1970, 47-year-old James Mitchell grew up with the signmaking trade. Unlike others in the industry who just seem to fall into a business and are not quite sure how or why it happened, James Mitchell has known what he was going to do with his life since the early 60's, when he befriended a signpainter who married the girl next door. Almost everything Mitchell has done since then has somehow involved signpainting. As a junior in high school, he painted signs for his art teacher. That same year, Mitchell learned to gild signs from one of the old gold leaf men, Art Johns, who used to brag that he had laid thousands of dollars of goldleaf (when it was $2.60 per pack) on the circus wagons headquartered in nearby Peru, Indiana.

Mitchell's interest in art led to his enrollment at the Fort Wayne Art Institute. As a fine art painting major, he learned about the principles of design, layout and composition. Not surprisingly, upon graduation, Mitchell blended back into the business he has always been a part of.

By 1970, the 22-year-old Mitchell was ready to hang out his shingle. He was so busy doing odd sign jobs, however, that he was in fact already in business. In the beginning he designed and lettered show cards.

As the years went by, Mitchell's repertoire and interest expanded. During the mid to late 70's, he worked the drag racing hub of the Detroit area. Pinstriping dragsters and funny cars was more than a job; it was a lifestyle. As the years rolled by, living out of a suitcase began to wear thin. And as Mitchell knew, "Sooner or later, another new young hot shot was going to move in."

By the mid 80's, Mitchell began concentrating his energies on intricate gilded and carved signs. Mitchell's local reputation gradually expanded once he began attending various Letterhead meets during the late 80's. As it has done for others, the Letterhead movement reinvigorated Mitchell's enthusiasm for the profession. That enthusiasm has spilled over into the 90's as Mitchell continues to make beautiful custom-crafted signs. His respect for the craft is evident by the designers he admires: Mark Oatis, David Butler, Noel Weber, Gary Anderson and the late great Mike Stevens, author of *Mastering Layout*. Mitchell learned a great deal from Stevens at the author's design workshop.

The more intricate and detailed the workmanship, the more Mitchell appreciates the design. Not surprisingly, although he admits to using vinyl signmaking equipment — "It's like having another employee" — clearly his heart is elsewhere. "It was such a great business before the computer came along," says Mitchell. "And it has put a lot of legitimate signshops scrambling."

Thanks in large part to his talent, Mitchell does not have to scramble for work. He does not have to make cold calls and rarely advertises. His portfolio and well-earned reputation are his primary selling tools. And if there is a gilded sign in Fort Wayne, chances are pretty good that Mitchell made it. After all, it's his life's work.

James Mitchell
Mitchell Signs

Recently I completed a samdblasted, carved and gilded balsa-wood sign. Why balsa wood? Balsa wood is an environmentally friendly commodity that is farm grown. Balsa trees can reach up to 100 ft. in 5-7 years. In addition, the wood is inexpensive, lightweight, durable and very workable.

With this project, carving is the key methodology. When gilding letters, you are at the mercy of the sign's environment to produce letter visibility. Flat, gilded letters reflect the color of their environment; sometimes appearing very bright, but at other times very dark. Carving the face of the letter into a slightly rounded configuration allows the letter to pick up and reflect light from virtually any angle. A carved, gilded letter can be read even at night if illuminated by just a nearby streetlight. Very little carving is required to achieve this effect, and the appearance can be quite dramatic.

Of fundamental consideration is the sign's design. I have chosen to use a more complex shape, based on a pyramidal format that suggests stability. (After all, what could be more stable than a pyramid?) I have placed the word "Blacksmith" — the most important of the three design elements in the sign — at the optical center. I use bold letters with collectively a very strong line value to push that line out toward the viewer.

Because the carved graphic — an anvil (symbolic of the blacksmith's trade) — is finished in a blue-gray, it appears to recede into the background.

The small copy — a less-important design element — is likewise "pushed back" by the use of a lighter line-value letter style and a finish of gray-blue (a color that relates more to the sign's background).

The size, shape, color and placement of the decorative wrought-steel details help resolve the stepped upper sides of the format into a pleasant, stable pyramidal shape. The three positive elements within the shape (the anvil, the word "Blacksmith" and the subordinate copy), plus the wrought hardware and the shape itself, mutually interact to create a pleasant composition. As in Gestalt theory: the whole is greater than the sum of its parts.

What follows is the step-by-step creation of the "Blacksmith" sign.

MAKING A BLACKSMITH'S SIGN

I begin by cutting the shape of the sign from approximately 2-in.-thick balsa wood. I have found that balsa wood can be worked nicely with very sharp hand and power tools. Even slightly dull tools have a tendency to rip and tear at balsa wood because of its lighter density.

Having sanded and primed the balsa, I apply and cut the sandblast stencil. I weed out the areas to be blasted.

When the letter surfaces are to be relief carved, it is very important to blast the sign straight on, so as to not undercut the letters. If, for example, the sand cuts in from the left or right and you carve the substrate down from the immediate surface, you lose the form of that side of the letter.

Once the sandblasting is finished and the stencil is removed, I begin the carving process by roughing out the basic contours with a riffler rasp. (These small, contoured rasps are available through woodworking supply houses.) Finer rasps work better with balsa; coarser rasps tear at the wood's soft grain.

I usually use diamond rasps because they are extremely sharp and cut in both directions of the stroke. By leaving a little of the primer showing in the centers of the letters, I can better see the contours and gauge the depth of my carving.

Having roughed out the carving with the rasps, I now blend and round the letter surfaces. The small amount of primed area that was left in the centers is now removed and blended into the edges. Doing so assures that there are no flat spots in the centers of the letters. Using a medium-grit sandpaper, this process goes quickly with the soft balsa. A sandpaper with a very sharp tooth, such as aluminum oxide or garnet, works best for this procedure.

Smoothing the surfaces of the border and the flat surfaces of the smaller copy with an orbital sander also goes very quickly.

The carved and sanded piece is now ready for finishing.

To achieve the super-smooth finish necessary for a brilliant gild, the letters must be finished with a sandable primer and sanded smooth at least three times using progressively finer sandpaper. I have never found a better material for priming than a product called FSC-88 (Finishing and Smoothing Compound). It was originally developed for priming and sealing high-density urethane and is available through Coastal Enterprises, Orange, California.

The primer can also be applied with a roller.

I prime and sand these letters five times because I want an especially smooth surface. The last sanding is done with a ScotchBrite pad.

Having primed and sealed all the lettering, I now paint the blasted areas with the best-quality exterior latex available. Latex paint moves with the expansion and contraction that occurs in all woods. I use three coats to protect the balsa from the harsh northern Indiana winters.

As the blasted areas are coated, I wipe the latex off the letter surfaces with a damp cloth to preserve the smooth finish I've worked so hard to achieve.

I use a yellow-tinted, slow oil size, which allows me to see that there are no holidays (small holes) in the size. Slow size sets to the proper tack in about 10-12 hours, holds its tack for many hours thereafter and produces a very brilliant gild.

The next morning, I gild the main copy. I use 23K loose goldleaf. I avoid patent leaf except when having to gild in the wind. Loose leaf yields a much more brilliant gild. I always burnish the gild with a very soft brush burnisher, never with cotton; cotton dulls the brilliance of the gold drastically.

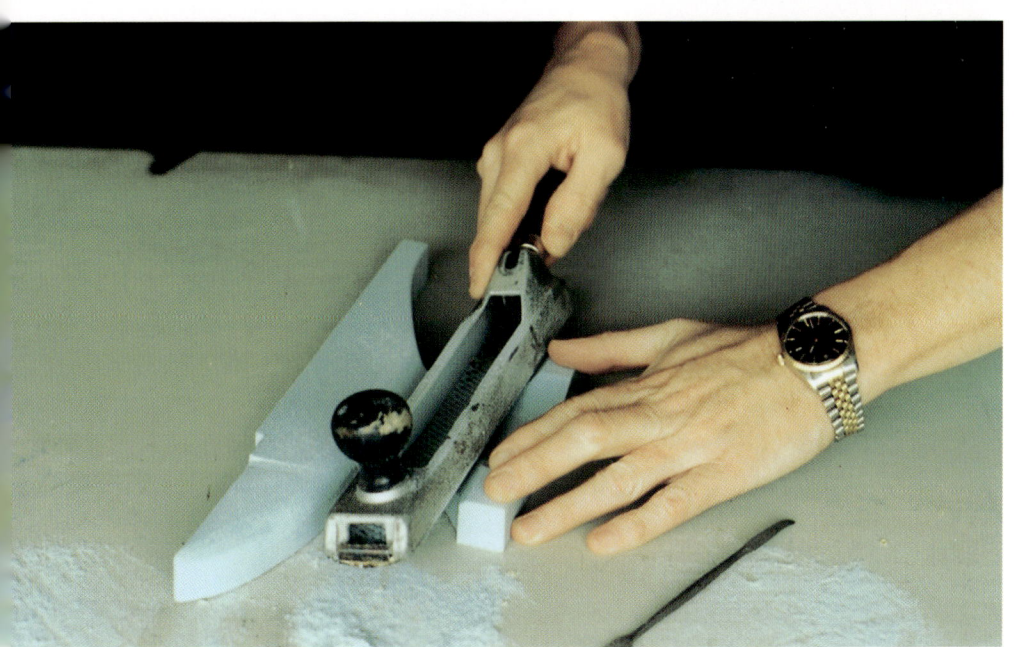

Having cut a silhouette of the anvil from high-density urethane, I rough-out the carving with rasps and sanding blocks. This material carves very easily.

Once the carving is roughed-out, it sands into great form, also very quickly and easily.

After priming, sanding and preparing the three-dimensional graphic (in the same fashion as I did the letters), I flow on a generous coat of lettering enamel.

Next, I coat the borders, edges and back of the sign with three coats of exterior latex.

MAKING A BLACKSMITH'S SIGN • 95

A pinstripe is added to reinforce the color of the small copy and to impart a subtle bit of color on the border.

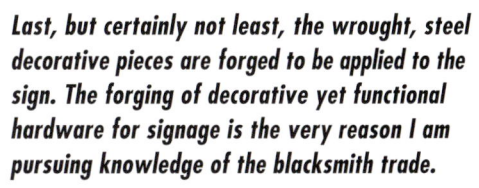

Last, but certainly not least, the wrought, steel decorative pieces are forged to be applied to the sign. The forging of decorative yet functional hardware for signage is the very reason I am pursuing knowledge of the blacksmith trade.

The finished sign.

MITCHELL SIGNS GALLERY

WOOD SIGN GALLERY • 97

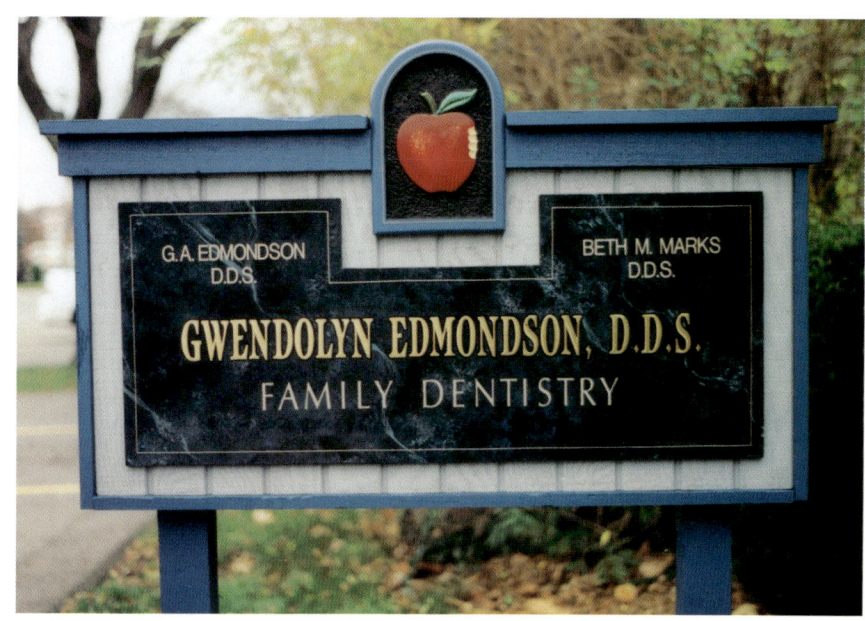

CONTENTS

10. Ina Brosseau Marx, Allen Marx and Robert Marx, *The Art of Graining* — 102

11. Bill Jonas, *Airbrush Sign Painting* — 114

12. Steve Chaszeyka, *Pinstriping* — 127

SECTION FOUR • *Paint*

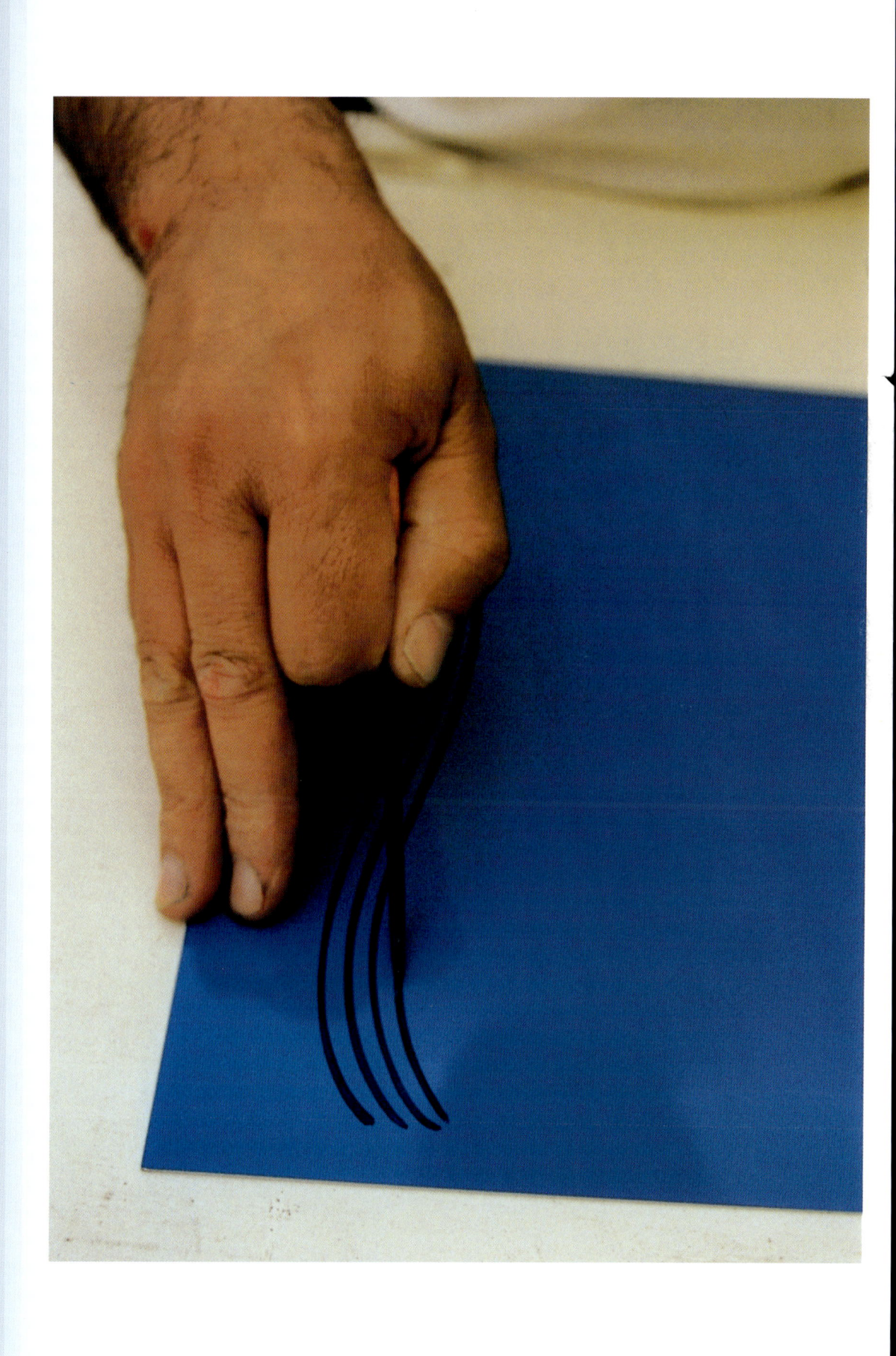

INTRODUCTION • Ina Brousseau Marx

The human eye, not being nearly the precision tool some make it out to be, is easily fooled. Magicians have long exploited the fact that their hands can move faster than the eye can follow. Printers print dots and the eye discerns picture. This inability of the eye to distinguish the forest from the trees has everything to do with faux finishing—making a painted substrate appear to be made of a material that it is not. In the world of faux finishing, illusion is reality. The eye sees a grained finish and tells the brain this is real wood.

Those who subscribe to the "faux" school have a place to call their own, The Finishing School in Port Washington, New York, where thousands of practitioners of the craft have taken one-day, two-day or week-long classes. The school was founded in 1981 and is directed by Ina Brosseau Marx, who has an impressive background in art and design, her husband, Allen Marx, and their son, Robert Marx.

The Marxes have devoted much of their lives to the subject of the painted finish. Besides teaching, the three Marxes have written a book on the subject, *Professional Painted Finishes,* and they produced a how-to video series as well. In addition, the Marxes have lectured extensively on the subject and conducted demonstrations for the Smithsonian, the National Decorating Products Association, the National Trust for Historic Preservation and many more. Their works are on permanent display at the Metropolitan Museum of Art and Yale University's Garvan Collection, among other places.

Allen Marx, Ina Brosseau Marx, and Robert Marx, The Finishing School

Although the time the Marxes have devoted to the subject is extensive, the time required to become moderately proficient in this aspect of decorative painting is relatively short. You do not have to be a professional artist to take a stab at the craft. The Finishing School has graduates from all walks of life, says Robert Marx. Amateurs may even have an advantage because they have not been trained in other painting methods. Explains Robert, "In many cases, people who have peripherally related skills seem to have an easier time learning the craft. Because we work with sponges and feathers and plastic and newspaper, people who have worked very hard to develop what we call fine art skills have to 'loosen up' and let go of a little bit of the control that they have worked so long to develop."

The idea in faux finishing is not to simulate nature as much as interpret it. "The best marble is not always the most realistic," says Robert. "You don't want to just copy it; you want to take the characteristics of a particular marble and create within those boundaries, evaluating it using good design principles." Ultimately, the feeling one is trying to achieve is a kind of structured disorder, a feeling of asymmetry, a pattern that is no pattern at all.

Three basic techniques for those who want to try their hand at faux finishing are glazing, marbling and graining. In its broadest definition, glazes are translucent films of colored media that are manipulated, while wet, over dried undercoats. Marbling and graining, are technically also glazes, but with specific simulated patterns of marbles and woods. The following chapter covers the technique of graining, achieving with paint the look of wood.

Faux finishing requires only the most basic of tools: various brushes, feathers, graining tools, sponges, paper, plastic, chamois, cheesecloth, household items such as pipe cleaners, toothbrushes, steel wool and even a potato to help remove paint media. There's a kind of unspoken tradition of coming up with new commonplace items

Allen Marx and Robert Marx

to simulate a various grain or stone effect. As many tools as there are, there are just about as many ways to manipulate them. Tools in faux finishing can be stroked, dragged, twirled, rolled, laid on, pounced on, pressed in, or used to spatter, whisk, blend, fuse or print.

The media includes pigments of many types, the liquid that carries the pigments (called the vehicle) and everything else that's part and parcel of each stage of decorative painting: lacquers, stains, varnishes, solvents and thinners. As always, the purpose of a medium is what it has always been: to decorate the surface, to protect it, and to keep it clean.

The quality of the various media, though, has changed dramatically over the years and this is very good news for signpainters. No longer do painters have to rely on using dangerous lead-based paints as developments in water-solvent systems such as latex-based house paint, acrylics, casein, tempera, and artists' watercolors have improved. New water-based products allow for the creation of a finish in one layer (which saves time) without the fumes. This quicker, easier method of reproducing faux finishes is a cost effective method and commercial signpainters should take note.

The faux finishing technique of graining is excerpted from *Professional Painted Finishes: A Guide to the Art and Business of Decorative Painting,* by permission of authors Ina Brosseau Marx, Allen Marx and Robert Marx, and the publisher, Watson-Guptill. The book is available from ST Publications Book Division, 407 Gilbert Avenue, Cincinnati, Ohio 45202, USA. Call 1-800-925-1100 or fax (513) 421-5144. A series of six companion videos—Marbling I and II; Marbling and Stones; Graining I and II; and Glazing—is available individually or as a set through The Finishing School, 334 Main Street, Port Washington, New York 11050, USA. Call (516) 767-6422 or fax (516) 767-7406.

Those seeking information about classes should also contact The Finishing School.

THE ART OF WOOD GRAINING

Graining, painting wood and *faux bois* are all names for the simulation of natural woods in any artistic medium. That simple statement describes what the ancient Chinese, Egyptians and Romans did thousands of years ago and what has been done since.

The challenge for grainers has always been to understand the structure of trees and the way trees are cut so that the grainers' renderings mimic authentic wood. Trees grow upward and outward, forming the familiar rings that mark yearly growth. These annual growth rings comprise a wide, light ring (spring or early-wood growth) and a narrower, dark ring (summer or late-wood growth). Whenever a tree is cut, the resulting grain pattern indicates the direction in which the cut was made in relation to the growth rings (and other portions of the tree).

In other words, any grain pattern in wood is a part of the tree from which the wood was cut and reflects the angle of the cut that exposed that part of the tree.

Fortunately for grainers, all trees have a limited number of cutting options. Thus, rendering woods becomes logical and accessible; specific cuts always reveal specific wood-grain patterns (see illustration on page 111). Hence, an analysis of tree structure and sawing methods provides a broad overview of the patterns available to grainers (more details will follow for particular woods). Using this information, you should be able to render many other wood grains.

Rendering grain patterns

Grain patterns can be created using applied or removal techniques or a combination of both. Choose applied graining technique when you need controlled placement of individual lines and toning. You may stop and start applied graining whenever you desire.

Removal techniques are used to produce an entire range of graining effects. These effects can be surprisingly realistic and have a natural quality that is difficult to obtain using applied methods. Just as with glazing, you must grain the entire taped-off board or panel while the glaze is wet.

The tools used in graining range from strie tools, used in glazing, to traditional graining tools, such as steel and rubber combs, rubber heels, pipe grainers mottlers and blending brushes (see photos on next page). Specific tools will be discussed with the techniques with which they are used.

Pore structure

The unique qualities of different pore structures — which in real woods range in size from fine to coarse, in shape from speck-like to linear, in coverage from sparse to dense and in color contrast from subtle to dramatic — are simulated in several ways. The following three techniques for creating pores are the most common: 1) flogging, 2) spattering and whisking and 3) steel-wool dragging (see photo on page 104).

Flogging

Flogging is a removal technique that produces an even layer of closely packed, separate, short (1/4 to 1/2 in.) strokes that cover the base coat completely. The tool used is a thin, wide brush with long, natural bristles called a flogger or dragger. If a flogger is unavailable, a natural-bristle housepainting brush can be used instead. Whichever brush is used, the final effect should look realistic, with all strokes crisp and vertically aligned. (See "Flogging Technique" on page 107.)

Flogging provides a "woody" background for any grain/pattern layer that is applied over it. However, flogging is especially effective when applied on a glaze that has already been broken up into randomly spaced light and dark streaks. Strie variations for producing light and dark streaks (such as the use of dry or glaze-saturated cheesecloth and the application of pressure) alter the visual texture of the flogging. Many woods without a defined grain pattern can be imitated simply by manipulating the toning layer(s) over a flogged surface.

Although distemper media (mostly beer) have been used for hundreds of years for flogging, other media may be used as well. Glaze formulas made with paint or stains are particularly suitable.

THE ART OF GRAINING • 103

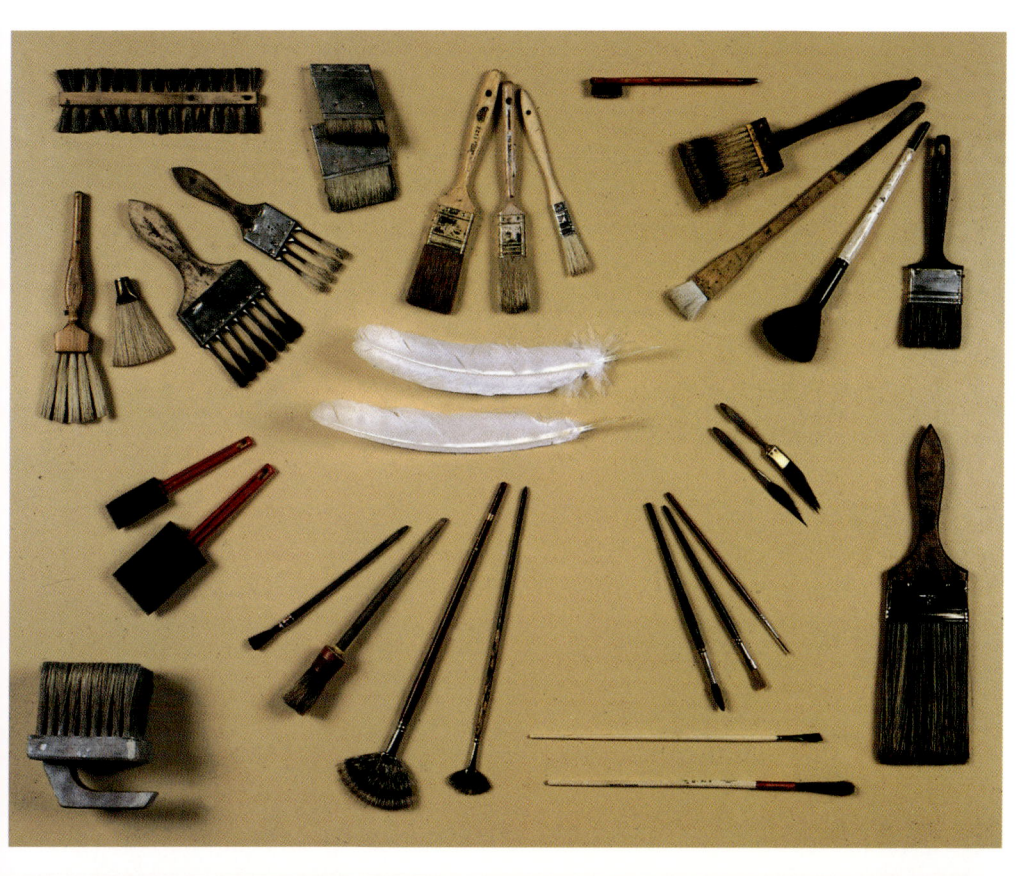

Brushes and feathers used in decorative painting: (1) two-side grainer (2) two mottlers (3) three stiff-bristled brushes (4) toothbrush (5) badger-hair blending brush (6) bake wash brush (7) mop (8) hog-bristle blending brush (9) walnut grainer (10) hand grainer (11) seven-part movable pipe grainer (12) four-part pipe grainer (13) two turkey feathers, cut and uncut (14) two sword stripers (15) two foam brushes (16) stipple brush (17) glue brush (18) stencil brush (19) two fan brushes (20) three artists brushes: hog-bristle brush, ox-hair brush and script liner brush (21) two liner and lettering brushes (22) dragger/flogger.

Tools used for removal techniques: (1) three rubber graining combs (2) heel (3) four rubber graining combs (4) torn cardboard square (5) notched cardboard square (6) two rubber window-washing squeegees (7) cotton swabs (8) four steel graining combs (9) wallpaper smoothing brush (10) pink eraser (11) green rubber eraser (12) rubber mucilage bottle cap (13) stump (14) two-sided wipe-out tool (15) two kitchen pot scrubbers (16) bronze and steel wool and (17) looped plastic roller.

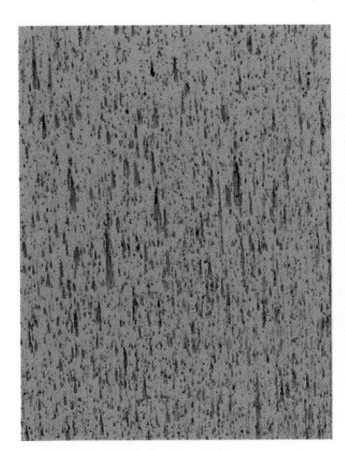

Comparison of pores created by three methods: (1) flogging (2) dragging steel wool and (3) spattering and whisking. Each technique was done with Benjamin Moore 1237 glaze over a Benjamin Moore 1063 base coat.

Making your own comparative stain charts over several base coats can be invaluable when selecting figure and toning colors.

Spattering and whisking

Spattering and whisking is an applied technique that simulates pores by creating 1/4- to 3/8-in. irregularly spaced fine streaks. This technique allows control of both the coverage (ranging from light to dense) and the quality of the pores.

To spatter, lightly load a spattering brush with a small amount of spattering media formula. The brush used to spatter can be any brush that is "springy" enough to flick off bits of media (toothbrushes or cut-off brushes, for example). Aim the loaded brush at a specific area and, with your index finer, flick the bristles slowly in succession. To avoid blotchy patches of spatter, keep moving your hand across the surface while flicking the bristles.

In addition to the consistency of the medium, other factors that affect spatter quality and density are how heavily the brush is loaded; the distance the brush is held from the surface; and how fast the hand is moved. Test the media consistency and your technique on scrap paper before spattering an actual working surface. The whisking process is done while the spatters are still wet. Flexible, stiff-bristled brushes (e.g., hog-bristle shellac brushes) are used to elongate and align the spatters. Hold the whisking brush so that the handle is parallel to the spatters and drag the brush along the direction of the grain. Select the size of the area to be spattered by determining how quickly the media drying and the whisking can be done.

Although flicking a brush is the spattering technique that offers the most control, you can also spatter media by moving a loaded brush along the teeth of a hair comb that is held parallel to the surface. Hitting a loaded brush against a piece of wood held a few inches from the surface works as well. There is also a tool made specially for spattering called a fuso machine; it's useful for those who spatter a great deal.

Spattering the media

Whisking the spattered media to produce pores

With the bristles held as parallel to the surface as possible, the flogger is slapped down and lifted up. Note the position of the wrist and the dragged texture of the yet-to-be-flogged section. The thin edge of the flogger can be used to realign the pores and fix other imperfections.

THE ART OF GRAINING • 109

Straight Grain Chart

This chart illustrates the wide variety of straight grains that can be achieved using various removal tools — from a nylon pot scrubber to traditional graining tools.

The selection of tools listed in this chart should by no means be considered definitive. In-studio experimentation (or "focused playtime") will no doubt uncover countless others that can be used. All of these examples were performed with a BM 1237 glaze over a BM 1110 base coat.

1) Horizontally pleated plastic, dragged once, with hesitation.

2) Dragger/flogger dragged once vertically. Pull the dragger/flogger across horizontaly when the glaze is almost dry. This technique is especially good for mahogany and satinwood.

3) Synthetic-bristled brush, dragged once.

4) Overgrainer brush, dragged once, with hesitation. This is especially good for walnut.

5) Ribbed carpet, dragged once.

6) Steel comb with 1/8-in. teeth, wrapped with the smooth (right) side of a stockinette and dragged once, with hesitation.

7) The sharp, 90° edge of a plastic-looped pot scrubber.

8) Flogger, dragged once vertically.

9) Triangular rubber comb dragged once vertically and, while the glaze is still wet, dragged again slightly off angle over the same surface. This technique works well for both American and quarter-sawn English oak.

10) The textured (wrong) side of a stockinette, crumpled, with many depressions. Heavy finger pressure must be used to create the lighter strips.

11) Steel comb with 1/8-in. teeth, wrapped with well-washed sheeting to absorb the medium. This is suited for homewood and sycamore.

12) Triangular rubber comb, combed once.

13) The smooth (right) side of a stockinette, crumpled, with many depressions.

14) Widely notched cardboard, dragged through several times then whisked lengthwise. Good for zebrawood.

15) Cheesecloth, crumpled with many depressions, then flogged.

16) The sharp, 90° edge of a synthetic sponge.

Analysis of Wood-Grain Patterns

The ability to render wood realistically depends heavily on understanding the various wood-grain patterns that typically appear (e.g., pores, straight grain, medullary rays, crossfire, heartgrain, ring cuts, knots, burl and the crotch figure (see illustrations on next page).

A lengthwise cut in hard wood reveals pores related to the tree's structure. Pores represent cut-open sections of the longitudinal cell structure of only hardwood trees. Soft-wood trees do not have pores. Diffuse-porous woods — like maple, birch and beech — exhibit evenly distributed small markings. Ring-porous woods — like oak, ash and hickory — exhibit alternating rings of larger and smaller pores.

Straight-grain patterns appear when a tree is divided lengthwise into quarters, when each quarter is cut into wedges and then each wedge is cut into boards. The end grain (grain at the end of the board) appears as straight, parallel lines. Also known as quarter-sawn, this straight-grain pattern exhibits the same variations in the widths and colors of the dark and light lines that are seen in the tree's annual growth rings.

Medullary rays, also known as silver grain, silver streaks, ray flecks and ray flakes, are food-storage tissues extending from the center of the tree out to the bark like the rays of the sun. Seen in quarter-sawn wood, medullary rays range from narrow and subtle to broader and more strongly marked. They interrupt the lengthwise pattern of the straight grain.

Crossfire, also known as mottle, is the reflection of light from wavy or interlocked grain. Interlocked grain results from twisting of the annual growth rings in alternate directions along the length of the trees. This occurs in many species — particularly tropical woods such as mahogany — that exhibit numerous crossfire figures.

Heartgrain, also known as cathedral grain, V-grain, plain sawn and flat sawn, is an annual growth-ring pattern of consecutive V-like shapes that are revealed when parallel vertical cuts are made across the width of a tree. Although trees seem columnar, they grow off-angle enough to provide many different heartgrain patterns.

When a tree is cut across the trunk — perpendicular to the length of the tree — the resulting pattern is called "ring cut." Also known as cross-cut and end grain, this pattern illustrates the annual growth-ring structure of a tree. The pattern comprises dark rings (the thinner, more-dense late wood or summer growth) and alternating light rings (the wider, less-dense early wood or spring growth). As the sapwood (the new rings that supply the tree's nutrients) is added annually along the tree's outer circumference, the heartwood (the older rings surrounding the center or pith of the tree) turns darker. Any cracks that form on the ring-cut always lead in toward the heart of the tree.

The patterns of knots vary with the way the tree is cut. Knots represent end-grain sections of a branch that the tree's annual growth rings eventually encapsulated. If the branch was growing diagonal to the tree trunk, the knot will be oval; if the branch was growing straight out of a tree, the knot will be round. Because a knot is a miniature ring-cut, it exhibits all ring-cut characteristics.

Burl, also known as burr figure, is wood from irregular growths on the outside of trees, cut to produce highly ornamental figures. Burls contain thousands of bud formations — would-be knots — and, in some species, a convoluted grain structure. Other species exhibit a pigmented mottling instead of grain lines. For decorative purposes, burl is cut as a veneer only because of its lack of lengthwise grain structure. The outer shell of a whole burl may be fashioned into a thick (up to 1-in.) bowl.

The crotch figure is wood that is cut from the section of certain trees where the central stem (trunk) has begun to form two limbs and exhibits strong patterns. This figure changes as the wood is cut farther toward the outer circumference of the tree. Also know as plume, swirl and feather figures, a crotch figure is a strongly contrasted pattern that looks like an upside-down rib cage. When a crotch figure is used decoratively, it is usually installed in the reverse manner from the way it is formed.

THE ART OF GRAINING • 111

Diffuse-porous

Ring-porous

Pores

Straight Grain

Straight Grain with Medullary Rays

Straight Grain with Crossfire

Heartgrain

Ring Cut

Knots

Burl

Crotch Figure

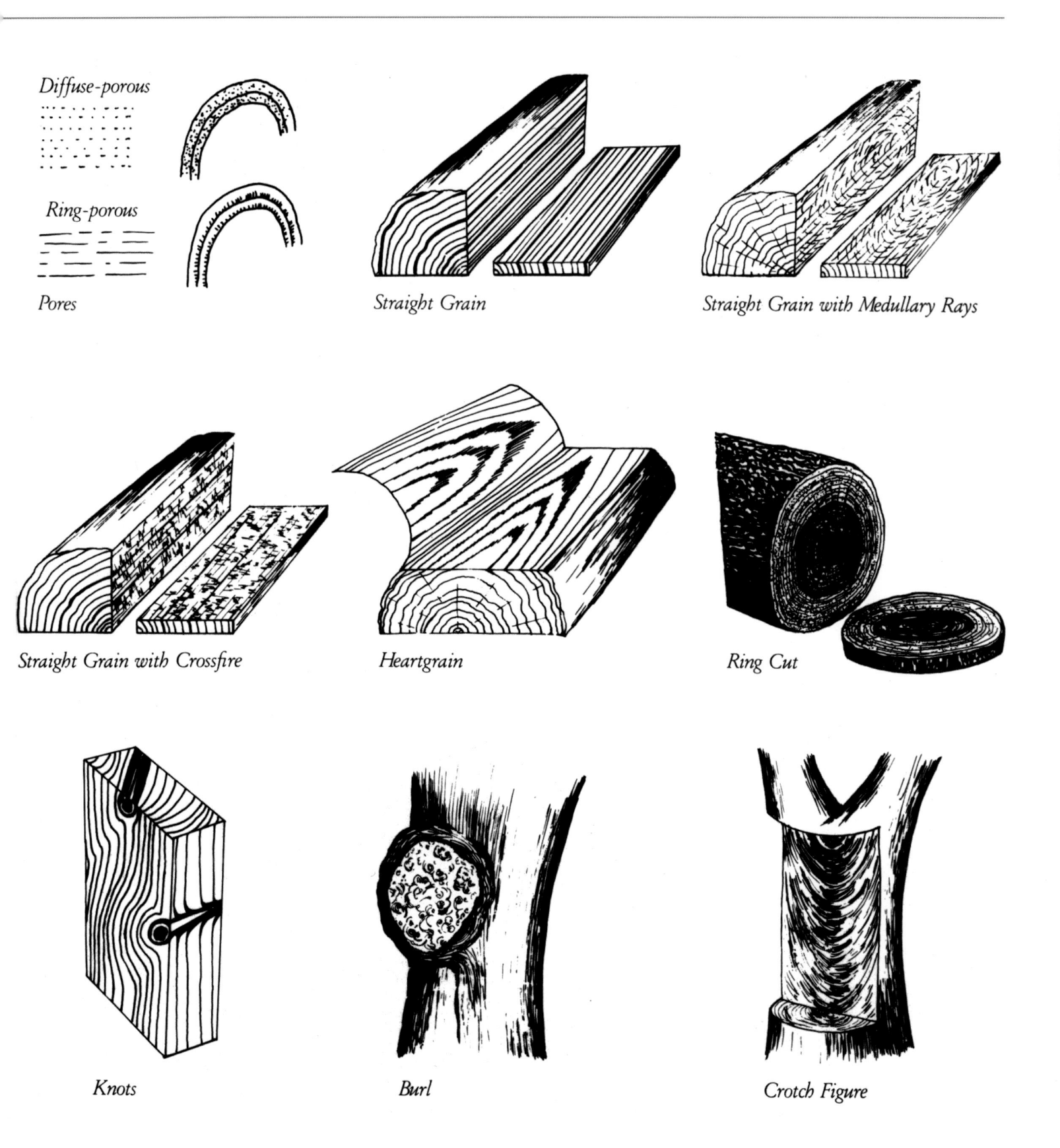

Wood grain patterns

INTRODUCTION • *Bill Jonas*

If you would have told Bill Jonas in 1971 that he would be the editor of *Airbrush* Magazine and one of the better-known airbrush sign artists in the country, he would probably have given you a strange look. (Although, to hear sign people tell it, that look is familiar to many in the industry who continue to be surprised at how they make their living.)

While Jonas always had an interest in commercial art, he did not drop out of school to paint signs. Instead, he was in a band and moved from northwest Indiana to the big city with the biggest shoulders: Chicago. Because he had an eye for commercial art, he also served as his band's artist; the one who designed the drum set and perhaps, some great day, its first album. However, when the band's equipment was stolen and there was no insurance, the band broke up.

Jonas' next job was nearly as fleeting: a summer gig for the government teaching Latino kids to paint murals rather than graffiti. Eventually, Jonas decided to use his mural knowledge to apply for a position at a signshop.

At Wing Sign Co., Chicago, — just five blocks from his house — owner Don Wing taught Jonas to hand-letter signs. For the next few years, Jonas paid for his "education" by hand-lettering "thousands and thousands" of signs for the housing-development market. Meanwhile, Wing's partner, Roy Toepper, taught Jonas the fundamentals of airbrushing vans; a skill Jonas was able to parlay into a career.

Bill Jonas
Airbrush Magazine

There comes a time when nearly everyone, with some skill and a drive to succeed, sets out on his own; Jonas' time came in 1981. Weary of the cold Chicago winters, Jonas headed to West Palm Beach, Florida, to set up a signshop. A salesman with whom he worked brought in the business quickly and, five years later, Jonas found himself running a 12-person operation; but not having fun. He had become a "businessman," not a signpainter, and he spent all his days immersed in paperwork and employee problems. Again, it was time to get out.

In retrospect, Jonas says, the money wasn't that good anyway. It seemed to Jonas, freelancing — working for and by yourself — was the way to go in the late 80s. "There was always just enough work to get by," Jonas remembers.

Jonas may have liked Florida's weather, but not the lifestyle. So in 1981, Jonas traded back Florida's weather for his friends and the comforts of Chicago. He returned to Wing Sign Co. for another stint and began doing what the mature Jonas believes was "very good work." So apparently, did others. For several years, he captured first-place slots in some airbrush contests and eventually his design skill captured the attention of the publisher of *Airbrush Action* magazine. The publisher asked Jonas to replace its recently departed editor in late 1991.

Jonas was in the right place at the right time; a new career beckoned in Lakewood, New Jersey. Magazine editing and publishing was a brave new world and, if Jonas didn't care for the business side of publishing, he became quite fond of the technical side. Each night after work, he "played" with the computer equipment. As with his airbrushing "education," most of what he learned on the computer was self-taught. Jonas lived up to his motto: "Don't be afraid to experiment; good judgment comes from experience; experience comes from bad judgment."

Once again though, Jonas missed the sign world. So in 1993, he left *Airbrush Action* magazine and started working at Twin Vision, Howell, NJ. His experience in the publishing world, however, left him with quite a few contacts. He was a regular contributor to a quarterly airbrushing newsletter until late 1993 when he was asked to help start up *Airbrush* Magazine — an offshoot of the Intl. Airbrush Assn. headquartered in Cosby, Tennessee.

Jonas had no illusions about the difficulty of starting up a magazine, but this was different: he did not sell ads; he was not the financier; and the business side was handled in another state. His job was well defined: he edited articles and provided the desktop-publishing support. Today, the quarterly magazine — in its fourth issue with a 25-30,000 print run — can be found in many art-supply houses.

Jonas says: "It's about time."

AIRBRUSH SIGN PAINTING

Project goals:

Design and fabricate a sign for display at the annual Sales and Marketing (SAM) awards for the state's housing developers.

Specs: Sign face is to be 5 ft. x 7 ft. and mounted on a black pedestal 18 in. high x 8 ft. long. The entire face of the sign is to bear the SAM logo large enough to be read from the back of the hall, yet elegant enough to befit the atmosphere of a black-tie event.

When we at Twin Vision, Inc., Howell, New Jersey, receive this assignment, our first thoughts are to do the logo as a large piece of sandblasted/etched glass. The glass would be mounted into the pedestal where it would be edge-lit from the bottom. However, the expense of the glass (or acrylic) makes it cost prohibitive. Likewise, a lighted sign cabinet leaves no room for labor costs. A painted sign is dismissed as too plain, but all of the fabrication routes are not feasible under the time and budget constraints.

Project Designer, Luann Lameiras, asks if it would be possible to "airbrush something to appear like fabricated metal." Because the main color scheme includes silver and gold, we decide the main lettering should look like silver with the state emblem in gold. The background color needs to be dark, but lighter than black (to make the airbrush shading show up), so purple is chosen.

Sometimes, painted signs are too easily passed by for a high-end option; we realize though, that with an airbrush and a little creativity, one can "fabricate" almost anything.

Step 1: Since the sign face is larger than a sheet of plywood, two sheets of MDO are seamed down the middle and attached to a wooden frame. The seam is puttied and sanded, and the entire face is primed. When the primer dries, it is scuffed, coated with white enamel and allowed to dry overnight. A low-tack paper frisket (used to transfer vinyl letters) is applied to the entire face of the sign. I make a pounce pattern of the lettering and pounce the design into place on the masking with charcoal powder. Next, I shift the pattern over and down a couple of inches to create perspective in the letters. This time, the pattern is pounced with blue-chalk powder, (blue represents the back; black represents the front of the letters).

To avoid accidentally wiping off the lines, I trace them with a felt tip pen. I draw the black pattern completely; the blue pattern is only drawn where it falls outside of the letters. Then, I connect all corners with straight lines to the corresponding corners on the other pattern. The point of view of the final lettering will change depending on the direction the pattern is shifted. By shifting the pattern up, for example, it will appear that the viewer is looking down at the lettering.

Rather than redraw all of the long lines across the face of the sign, I run masking tape to serve as a cutting guide. All of the lines are cut with a stencil knife before the painting begins. Otherwise, the lines would get covered with paint overspray and be obscured or completely lost. I am careful not to cut deep into the MDO; so that the masking paper cuts easily, I use a fresh blade.

Step 2: The background is to be purple. So, I peel off all areas that indicate background. To cover larger areas, I apply the enamel with a short-nap roller. I use the paint as sparingly as possible to cover completely. Too much paint would make the masking difficult to peel away without tearing up the edge.

AIRBRUSH SIGN PAINTING • 115

Step 3: After the background is rollered in, I use black in the airbrush to create a soft shadow next to each letter.

Step 3 (detail): I make the shadow darker than a natural shadow to exaggerate the illusion of dimension. (It is often necessary to exaggerate certain effects to make them more effective, especially where lighting conditions or distance detract from visibility.)

Step 4: The lines that cross the logo in its two-dimensional form, now become shelves on which the letters sit in the three-dimensional form. With this design, there are no bottoms of the letters to paint, only a long shelf broken by the tops of the letters on the next line. I remove all of the masking on the bottom of the shelves first (since that will be the darkest area). To make it slightly more transparent, I thin down the black in the airbrush. By doing this, any overspray that may get on the purple won't be noticeable.

Step 5: Next, I remove the masking covering the bottoms of the serifs. These areas would technically be the same shade as the bottom of the shelf that they are against, but, since they are part of the letter, they are instead left a bit lighter so they will not blend into the shelf. I leave a distinct line where the two planes meet.

Step 6: The sides of the letters are now peeled, revealing a sharp contrast between the dark airbrush and the white board. Because everything under the masking is pure white, I want to be sure everything that gets painted in will be dark enough to contrast. Also, I want to make sure all exposed areas get at least some spray so the edge will contrast against the white that is still masked.

I realize the thinned down black in the airbrush will cover the white quickly, but will be hardly noticeable on the previously painted shadows. For this reason, I plan my airbrush masking work from the darkest to the lightest shades, peeling all of the areas of the same shade at the same time. I can accomplish a lot of depth by adding very little spray. Also, because this method doesn't require any remasking, the painting can be completed without the delays of allowing the paint to dry between steps.

Step 7: When I color the sides of the letters, I take special care to leave a good amount of contrast at the corners (where the side meets the bottom of the serif). The corners are important because that is the visual information that gives the illusion of depth. I want the sides of the letters to remain lighter than the bottom of the shelf, but also be darker than the white under the masking.

Step 8: *The secondary lettering is added with a stencil cut on a computer-driven plotter. The plotter holds a small knife blade that cuts images into a sheet of adhesive-backed vinyl. Any images — graphics or lettering — that are drawn on the screen are sent to the plotter, and cut at actual size into the vinyl. The vinyl is then registered in position and adhered to the painting surface. In this case, the vinyl letters have been removed, leaving only the vinyl background as a mask. Now, with a short-nap roller, I apply the color very sparingly.*

Once the lettering is completely filled in, I remove the masking. Then I allow 10 minutes or so for the enamel to tack so the masking doesn't pick up long strings of wet paint; I don't let the paint dry completely though, because the masking may peel up the dry paint.

Step 9: *I lightly airbrush the panels behind the secondary copy with strokes of thinned-down black, staying back from the surface for a wide-spray pattern. Since the purple lettering is much darker than the mist of color that is being sprayed, the overspray does not visually affect the letters.*

Step 9 (detail): *After toning the background of the panels with a metallic effect, I airbrush the black next to the letters for a shadow effect. After that, I add white to the opposite side as a highlight (to make the lettering appear to be embossed). As a final touch, I add a white horizon line across the center of the face of the lettering and graduating upwards slightly. This makes the lettering appear to be shiny.*

Finally, I remove the masking from all of the lettering. I want the lettering to remain white, because when airbrushing is applied properly, the letters stand out well against everything else that is in the background.

Step 10: The only part left to be painted is the graphic shape of the state of New Jersey. Since this area is a different color, I have left it for last. First, I remove the center of the masking, leaving a wide border separating the graphic from the background colors.

Since this emblem is to appear as gold metallic, I give it a basecoat of a medium gold color. There is a wide border of masking, so I can use a roller to coat the area. While the paint is still wet, I airbrush a darker shade (gold with brown) at the top, fading down to the gold color in the center. Then, I add a lighter shade (gold and white) at the bottom, so that the entire area fades from dark gold at the top to light gold at the bottom, with a good amount of the original color left in the center. Because it is important that the color fades evenly from one shade to the next, when necessary, I mix a little of the original gold in the airbrush, and soften the transition zones. This color gradation gives a metallic effect from a distance, and the overspray outside of the masking is negligible.

Step 11: I remove the piece of masking left around the state graphic and apply various shades of gold and brown with a brush to suggest a beveled edge around the graphic. By keeping the light source in mind (upper left, in this case) I add the lightest shades to the upper right surfaces, and the darkest shades to the lower right surfaces. With the brush, I paint in the various planes around the graphic. I then blend these together with the airbrush. Employing the same colors in the airbrush, I use the neighboring colors to highlight and shadow each section and blend it into the next. I keep the airbrushing to a minimum, and mostly work well inside of the painted stripe; airbrushing too close to the edges would cause noticeable overspray. Adding highlights and shadows to the center of the strip is enough to carry the illusion of dimension without getting too detailed.

Step 11 (detail): *Now's the time for me to finish up the outline treatment (airbrush highlights and the shadows are added freehand). I keep star highlights to a minimum for the best effect. I create them by spraying along the edge of a piece of paper, then turning the paper 90° for the second pass, and finally, spraying a large highlight in the center.*

I allow all of the paint to dry overnight. The next day, I roller on a clear coat of matte-finish polyurethane to prevent the stage lights from glaring on the surface.

The finished sign.

AIRBRUSH GALLERY

AIRBRUSH GALLERY • 121

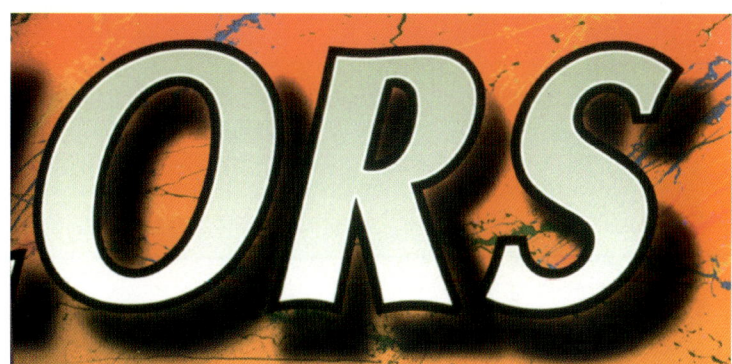

122 • SECTION FOUR • PAINT

AIRBRUSH GALLERY • 123

124 • SECTION FOUR • PAINT

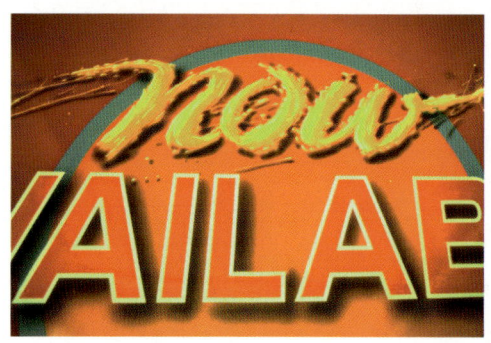

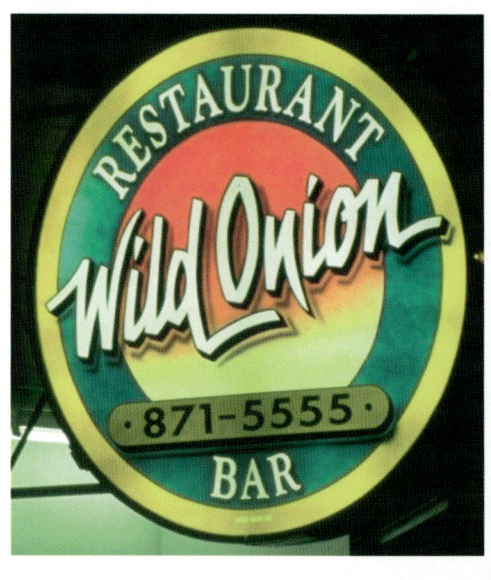

AIRBRUSH SIGN PAINTING • 125

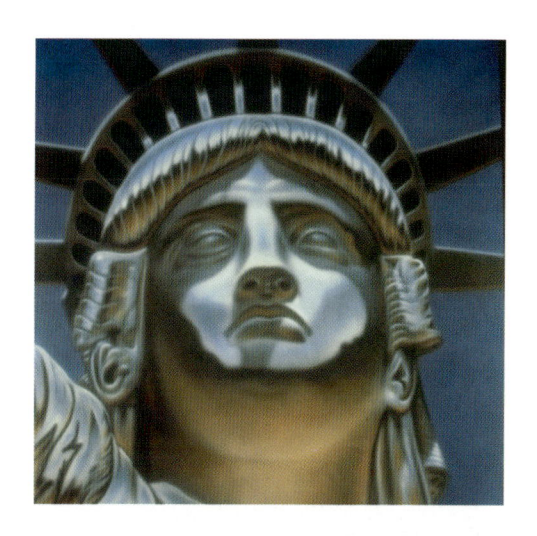

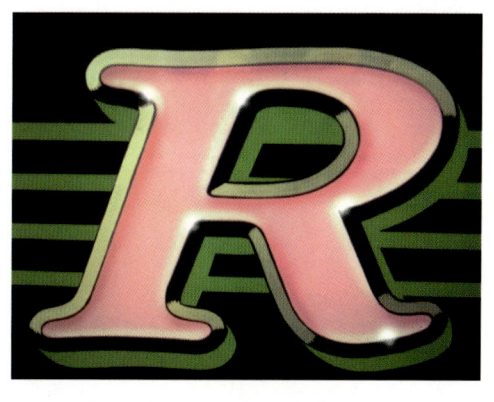

INTRODUCTION • *Steve Chaszeyka*

By his own estimate, Steve Chaszeyka's got to practice a lot more before he'll finally have his straight lines to the level he wants them. No matter, really. The pinstriper who has run Wizard Graphics out of New Middletown, Ohio, for the past seven years has always valued practice.

Ever since Chaszeyka started satisfying his "need for attention" by drawing cartoons in the first grade, he knew he'd wind up doing something artistic. All the jobs that he took were mere prologue to the pinstriping work he was going to produce. During a ten-year period in which he sold insurance with his father, he had more success selling signs and vehicle graphics to his customers than the insurance. A new business was born. When one of those customers—an ex-pinstriper—actually hired him to work at his art studio, the insurance business was left behind and suddenly Chaszeyka found himself heading up his own mail-order department, designing motorcycle decals.

For a time, it was heaven for Chaszeyka. He worked at that studio for several years, all the time picking up work on the side, painting stripes on any flat surface he could find: refrigerators, shelves, lawnmowers. Combining his growing confidence in going out on his own as a full-time pinstriper with some unresolved office politics, he left the studio. And despite his boss's challenge that he wasn't organized enough to succeed, Chaszeyka managed to hustle his way to gross $100,000 in his first year. Not all profit of course. He had to pay for materials, overhead and travel to car and bike shows. But the business thrived, even in depressed Youngstown, Ohio.

To pinstripe a bike or car usually runs $125-150 and it takes 60-90 minutes of work. "When you get to the end of the line and have to produce a design, that's what people will pay for. They'll pay the big bucks for that." According to Chaszeyka, speed is not a factor in pinstriping. Yes, it will allow you to produce more work, but sometimes at the expense of accuracy. "Seventy five percent of the show guys can go faster and straighter than me," he says. "But I blow them away on the designs." Those who have scouted around from shop to shop often come back to Chaszeyka. He's generally considered one of the very best pinstripers around "It's a great feeling to have a $50,000 street rod owner bring his rod to you and say, 'What would you do with this?'"

Chaszeyka protects his craft like a mother protects her baby. "If you want to learn pinstriping, for goodness sake, don't grab a disk and a four-inch roller and call yourself a pinstriper. Pick up a double ought Mack and a can of One-Shot and go out there with a panel." According to Chaszeyka, there is but one way to learn pinstriping: practice. Chaszeyka offers his "rule of thousands:" pull a thousand straight lines. Then pull a thousand verticals, a thousand right hand "S's", left hand "S's" and semicircles. The test is one of endurance that most beginners fail.

"What most guys do is they pull 30 or 40 of the lines and they say, 'Well, I'm ready to do a car.' Then they go out and butcher up some cars." Only through practice will one truly learn the craft, earn the "hand" that pulls curves as easily as straights. Even Steve Chaszeyka continues to practice his straights at every opportunity.

Steve Chaszeyka
Wizard Graphics

PINSTRIPING

The tools and materials required for pinstriping: brush, paint, thinner, masking tape, and cleaner.

Use a new razor blade to trim less than 1/32 of an inch in an upward direction. The idea is to flatten the point of the brush. Extraneous hairs will interfere with the exact width of your stripe.

We're going to need brushes, paints, a straight-edge razor, materials to clean the vehicle before you stripe it, something to palette on, and some tape to give yourself a guideline. Brushes come in a wide variety of styles and designs.

The smallest number of hairs are 00 (double ought) and they increase in size to 0, 1, 2, 3, 4 and 5. It is interesting to note that although the number of hairs in the bristle may change, the length of hairs will vary by manufacturer. The cost, too, can vary enormously depending upon the quality of the bristles, the type of handle, and in general, the overall quality of the brush itself.

In addition to the number of hairs on striper brushes, there are any number of types of brushes and handles that can be used. Types of brushes include a chisel point (sometimes called an outliner) a sword, a dagger and taper. The outliner is generally used for curlicues while the others are used for the more traditional straights and curves and decoratives. Either square handles or curved handles are used by pinstripers, the theory being that square are used for straight and curves for curved lines. In truth, I rarely (if ever) use a square handle. It is, though, a matter of taste, as is the grip.

There are, by the way, mechanical brushes which go by various names, such as Buegler Stripers. These mechanical stripers have movable tips with varying width and can "roll" stripes ten times the speed of a brush. For certain production jobs (for a truck line for example) these stripers are highly recommended. One reason is that they paint lines nearly three times as thick. Trucks painted with these stripers can withstand high pressure, multiple washings.

When storing your brushes, there are two accepted methods: wet or dry. I prefer to store brushes wet, cleaning out the brush with turpentine and then using some form of lubricant to keep the bristles wet. Others prefer the dry method which usually means blotting the bristles on a cloth until dry. In my opinion, the dry method risks having bristles appear too blown dried, just like what happens to your hair. Unruly blown dried bristles are not what a pinstriper wants. Others, however, disagree. It's a matter of preference. One final note about brushes: the cost of the brush is not really indicative of the quality. I recommend going with a Mack; it's cheap and it works. Besides, once you have worked the proper technique, a good pinstriper can use a Q-tip.

For a starter, the safest brush to use is probably a 00 Mack. This brush has a nice feel to it, a nice grip. It is easily maneuverable, not a specialty brush that has a singular purpose, such as a straight line, flattened or sharp. The Mack has a round handle which allows you to roll it and turn it as you make curves, but it also has a pleasant enough shape that when you pull a straight line, it will respond to a nice, straight line. The reason we start with a 00 Mack, as opposed to a 1, 2, 3 or 5 is that generally most customers want a thin line on their cars. I can use a 00 Mack to pull a 1/4-inch line down the side of a car as easily as a 1/64-inch line down the side by just releasing some of the pressure as I pull. The 00 Mack has a great deal of versatility. To begin with, you might want to buy two or three of these brushes because we are going to trim this brush; if you make a mistake on the first try, you will have a second brush to work with.

The idea is to trim only the extraneous tips of the hairs working outward toward the tip. You will need to open one of the cans of paint or your brush oil, and dip your brush in the oil or paint, and pallet it out. To pallet a brushload of paint, simply smooth it out on a piece of notebook paper or phone book paper. The desired result is to get this sword brush to flatten out. You will notice on the tip of the brush there are a few pinpoint hairs that stick out, providing a very, very fine point. Trim those few little hairs 1/32" or 1/64" off the end of the brush.

The reason we do this is that in the design aspect of pinstriping, lines are connected to form designs. It's very important that these connections come to a point and butt closely together without overlapping or leaving jagged edges. Overlaps and jagged edges make your work look sloppy. Trimming a brush down just this very little bit modifies the tool with which you are able to connect these lines cleanly.

Clean your brush and oil it and then we will discuss how to begin pulling straight lines. I am going to introduce you to the teaching method that I have devised called "The Thousand Stroke Method." You're going to need substrate to paint on. I recommend 12 x 18-inch pre-painted aluminum panels. The surface or "tooth" of aluminum baked finish panel is very similar to that of an automobile. It provides just the right amount of drag that you will need.

As a practice panel, I prefer not to work on glass. Even though glass is very easy to clean off with a razor blade, it does not come as close to the surface of the painted vehicle you will eventually be working on. So, try to get yourself several aluminum panels to work on. If you can't find or order aluminum panels, real estate signs work well, too. You can also go to the junk yard and get an old car door or hood or trunk lid to work on. Just make sure it still has a shiny surface.

Don't do as I did and start striping cabinet doors in the house. This makes the rest of the family very uneasy about your job.

You'll also need a roll of 1/4" or 1/16" masking tape to use as a guideline, some clean cotton rags, not polyester, some mineral spirits (a gallon of regular turpentine works just fine), and some One Shot lettering enamel (or another brand of Chromatic paint). You're also going to need automotive degreaser. Sometimes it's called wax remover or pre-cleaner. This is necessary to remove wax, silicones, hand prints and grease from the surface, and provide good adhesion. If the surface is not cleaned sufficiently, the paint will come off because it is applied in such a small, thin amount. Once all the materials are in order you can begin to develop your hand.

When pinstriping, it's very important to develop "muscle memory." This involves the process by which you train your eye and your hand to work together to produce a line that is consistent, thin and straight every time. This is not going to happen the first few times you pick that brush up and put it in paint. Nor the second time. Developing muscle memory takes lots of practice.

Our practice involves taking the 1/4-inch tape and moving to the left side of the panel, about an inch from the left edge, and laying a strip of tape down from the top to the bottom of the panel, about an inch from the border. Add some thinner to your paint. The consistency of the paint is very important at this point. The consistency has to be wet enough so that it won't drip off the brush and has to be dry enough so that it doesn't clog or skip as you pull it down the panel. Try to get the paint the consistency of a syrup. If it's too thin, it will run like milk; if it's too thick, it won't spread out. When you get just the right consistency, you will eventually be able to pull a 3- or 4-foot line with one brushload of paint.

Conditions such as temperature and humidity will vary when you are painting. If it's a hot, dry or windy day, the paint will dry a little quicker and you may need to thin it a little bit more. On a cold day paint will dry more slowly, so you may need less thinner. If you load your brush straight out of the can, without any thinner, you may get an extremely thin line, but the paint will dry on the brush. You eventually have to add thinner anyway.

You need to keep those brush hairs saturated through and through all the time. If the brush begins to dry you are liable to become inconsistent. So, my advice is to dip your brush in correctly thinned paint and "lick" it back and forth on your palette until you get the brush saturated with paint. Not dripping wet, just full of paint. You need to palette this back and forth a good dozen, maybe two dozen, times, just to get the right consistency on your brush.

One way to hold the brush is the "two-finger grip," with the thumb and forefinger holding the brush while the little finger is used as a guide.

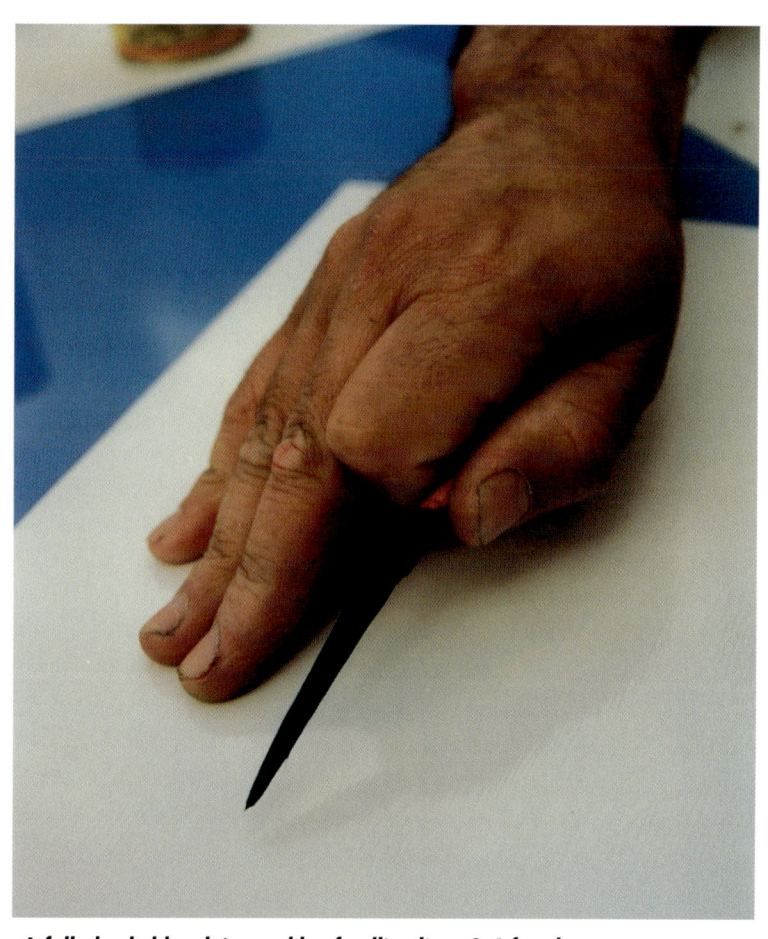

A fully loaded brush is capable of pulling lines 3-4 feet long.

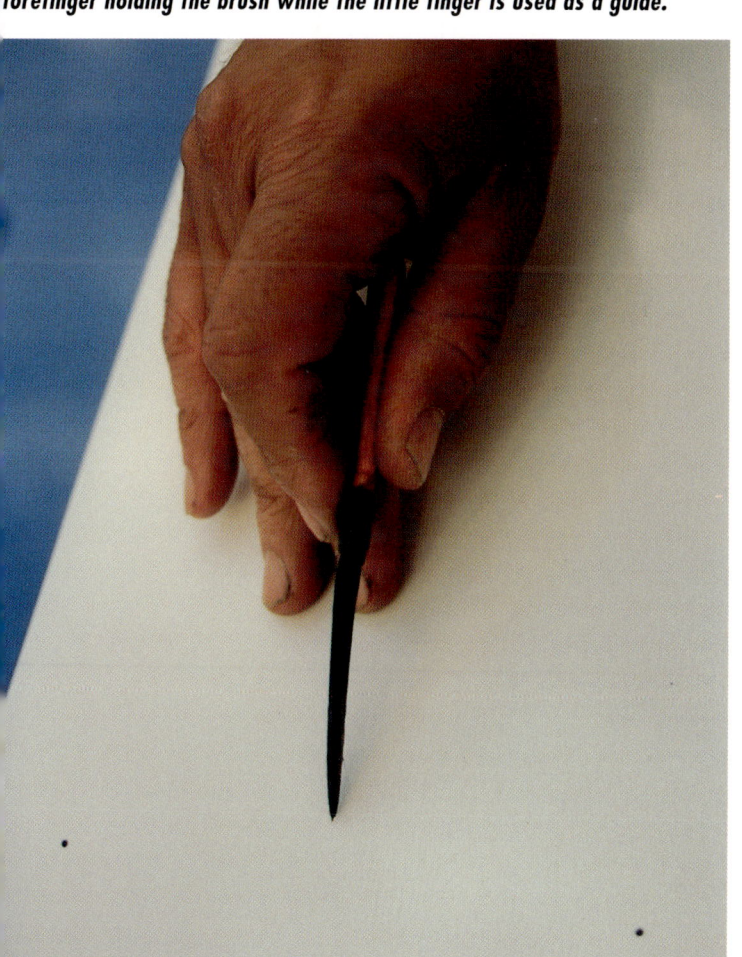

The two-finger grip works well on straight lines.

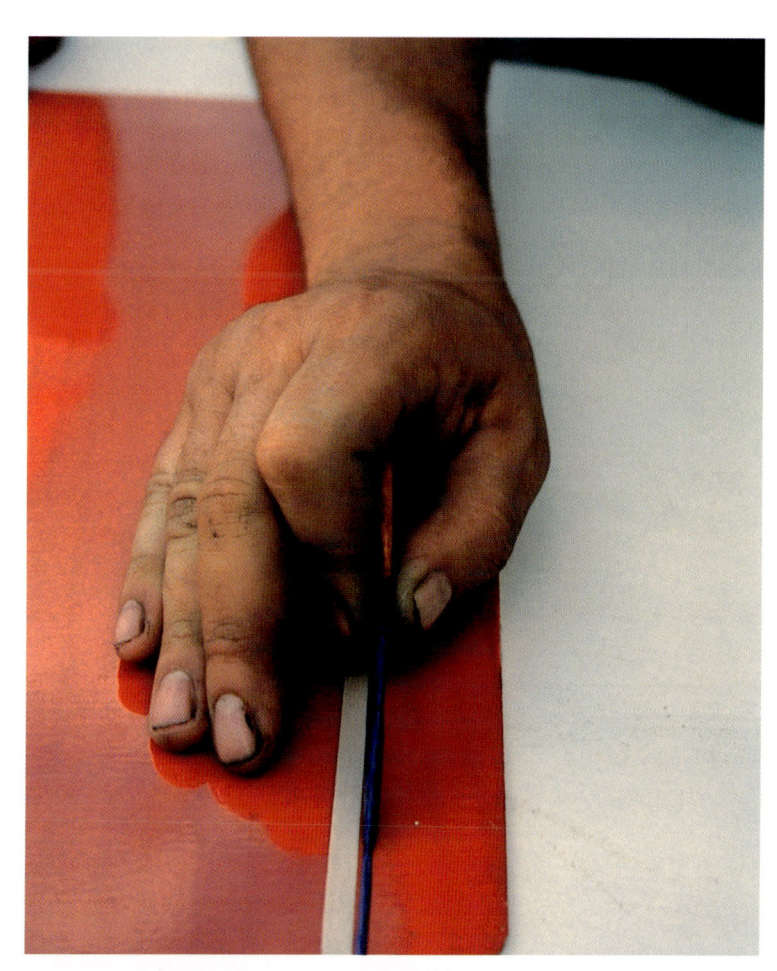

Practice by placing a 1/4-in. masking tape 1/2 an inch from the edge of the panel and pull the first line along the tape.

There are several grips that can be used. The two most often used both have the thumb and forefinger as the actual control element with either the little finger as the guideline or all three remaining fingers as the guidelines. You may want to try to adjust your grip from time to time to see what grip feels better for you. You're at the beginning stages now; it doesn't matter if you change your grips.

Now, taking your brush over to the substrate or panel that you have prepared with tape, go to the left side of the tape and choosing your grip, begin on the top of the line and pull to the bottom of the line, trying to stay as parallel with that tape line as possible. Leave that line on that panel because we are going to use this as a reference point. After you've pulled a number of these lines, go back and check your leader lines with your first line and see the progress you've made.

Make a series of lines from top to bottom — vertical lines — and try to stay about 1/4" apart. Do this 100 times. If you can't get 100 lines on that panel, wipe them off with thinner and a rag, being careful not to wipe off your first line, then clean your panel and start again. Don't go to a separate panel. Try to stay on this panel. When you're ready to pull your 100th line, put it next to your first line. You'll see a marked difference: within 100 strokes, hopefully, you'll make a great deal of progress. Repeat this process, marking each 100th line, all the way up to 1000. This is what I call "The Thousand Stroke System." It may seem boring, it may seem tedious, it may seem routine. But when you're on a job you don't want a challenge in getting a line straight. You want to be able to pull a line routinely, from muscle memory.

After your 1000th vertical line, you are ready to do a horizontal line. The horizontal line is one of the most consistently used lines in the pinstriping business. Lay the tape sideways now, just an inch in from the edge (as before) and pull horizontally. This might come a little easier than your first vertical line because you have begun to develop control of the brush a little bit. You still require a thousand strokes — don't cheat yourself. Leave your first horizontal line on the panel and, pull your 100th line below it. Work your way up through 200, 300, 400 (again, as with the verticals), marking each 100th line in a series so that you can see the progress and begin to develop horizontal muscle memory.

Now that you have learned the routine of The Thousand Stroke System, we need to move on to the decorative lines. There is the C-curve, the S-curve, and the vertical and horizontal C-curve and S-curve. Quite a few more lines to practice, but the drill remains the same. You can take your tape off for the decorative, curvy lines, but you still need to pull your first line on the side of the panel and your 100th through 1000th.

For curves, you will need to learn how to hold and turn the brush differently. For wide turns, you will hold it at perhaps 40° to the surface. For a very tight turn, though, you pick up the brush and hold it at a nearly 90° angle with the tips of the hairs just barely touching the surface. You can then roll the hairs of the brush.

I cannot say you will have creative ability and talent enough to make exotic designs, but I know that you will be able to pull some nice straight lines. You may be uncoordinated and need 2000 strokes or 10,000 strokes, but to this very day, I enjoy picking up a brush and practicing myself, so don't think you'll ever be through practicing.

When you practice in this manner, you will be able to see your progress.

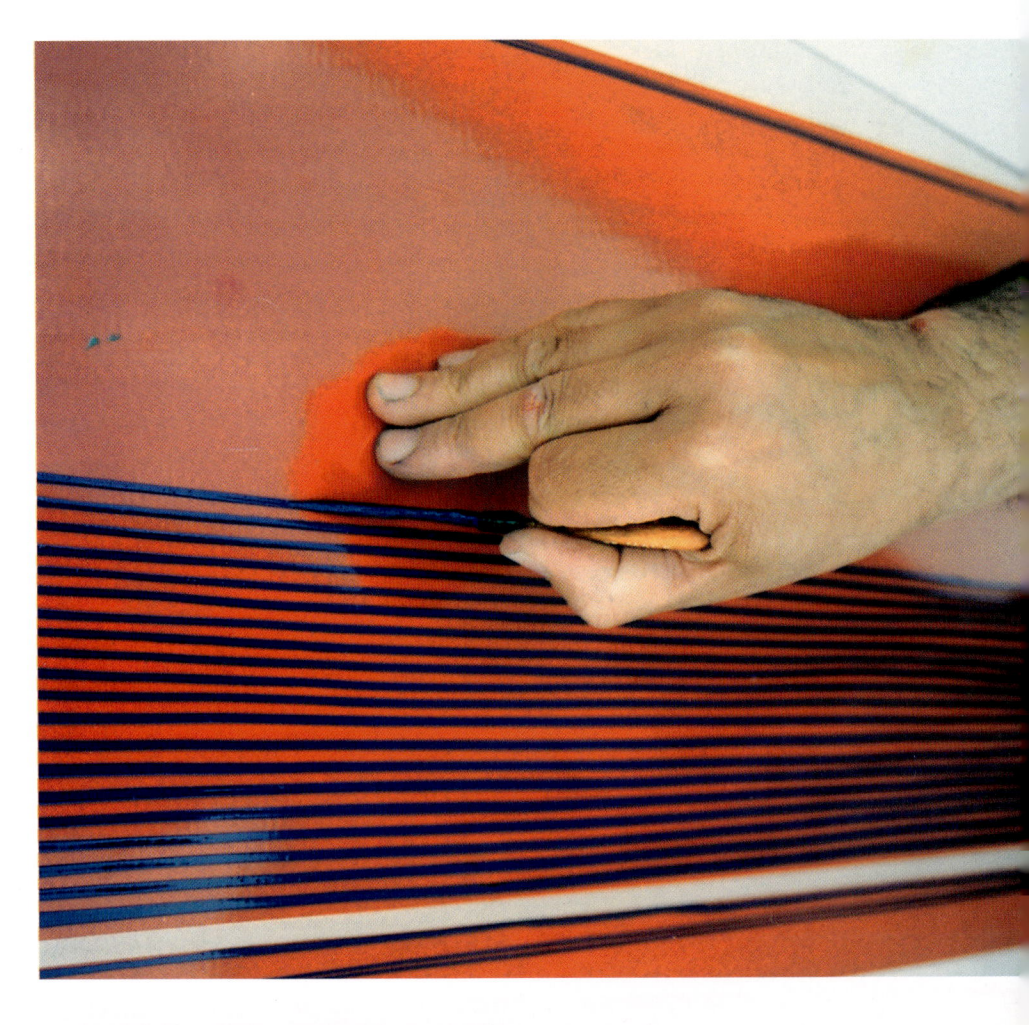

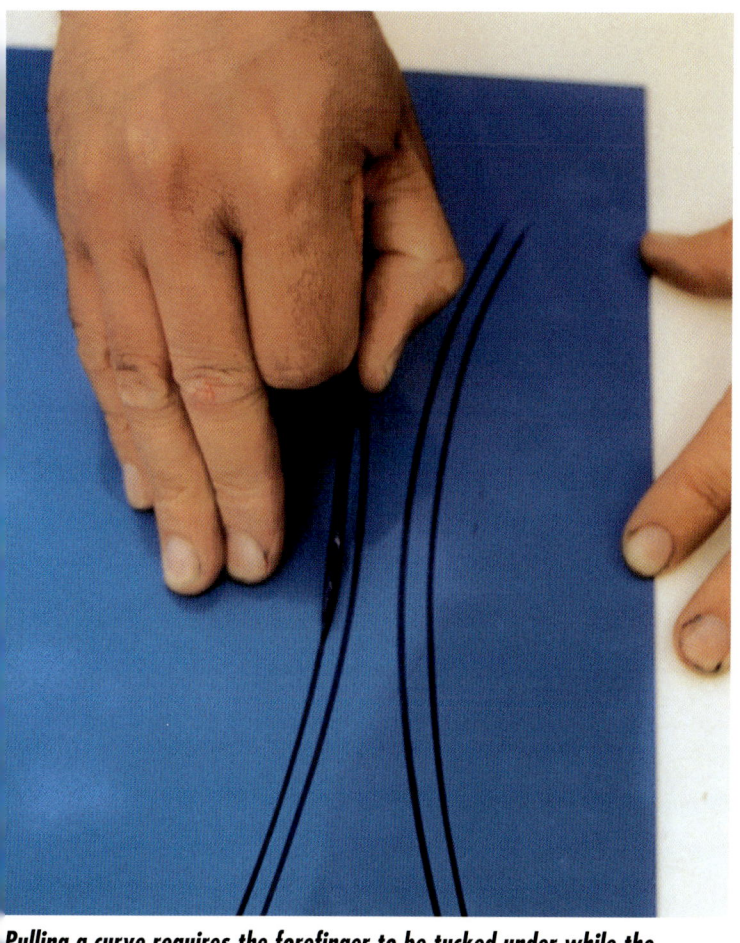

Pulling a curve requires the forefinger to be tucked under while the remaining three fingers act as a guide and support.

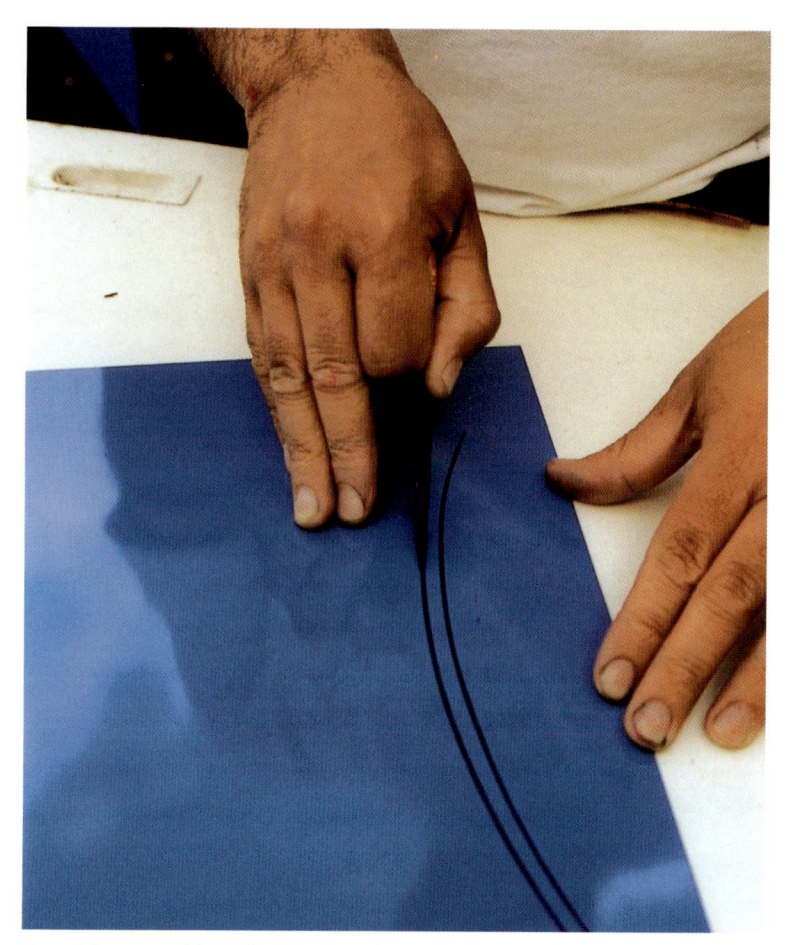

Practicing curved lines does not require using tape.

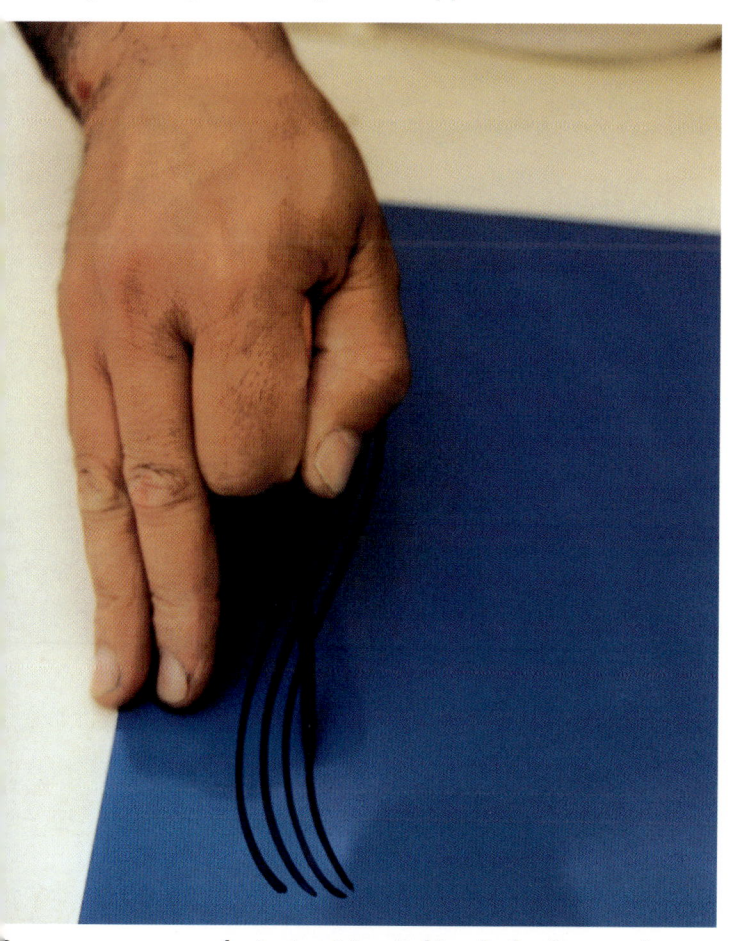

S-curves are very popular in pinstriping. Tucking the forefinger under allows for easier manipulation around the curves.

These are the types of curved lines you should practice.

PINSTRIPING GALLERY

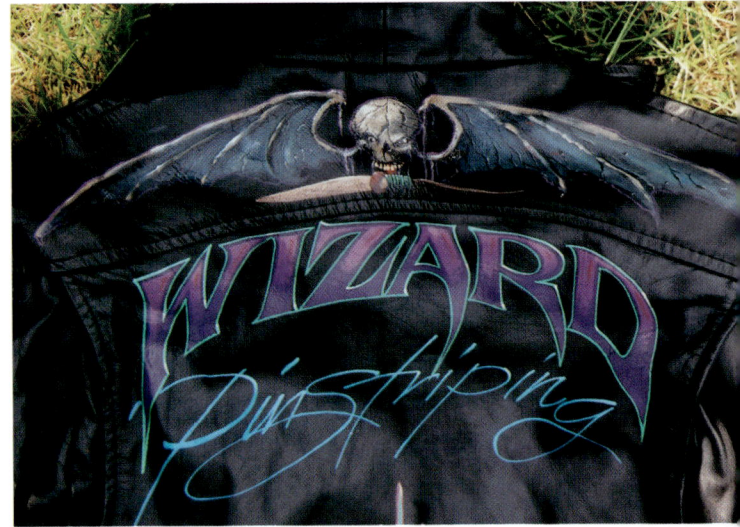

AIRBRUSH SIGN PAINTING • 133

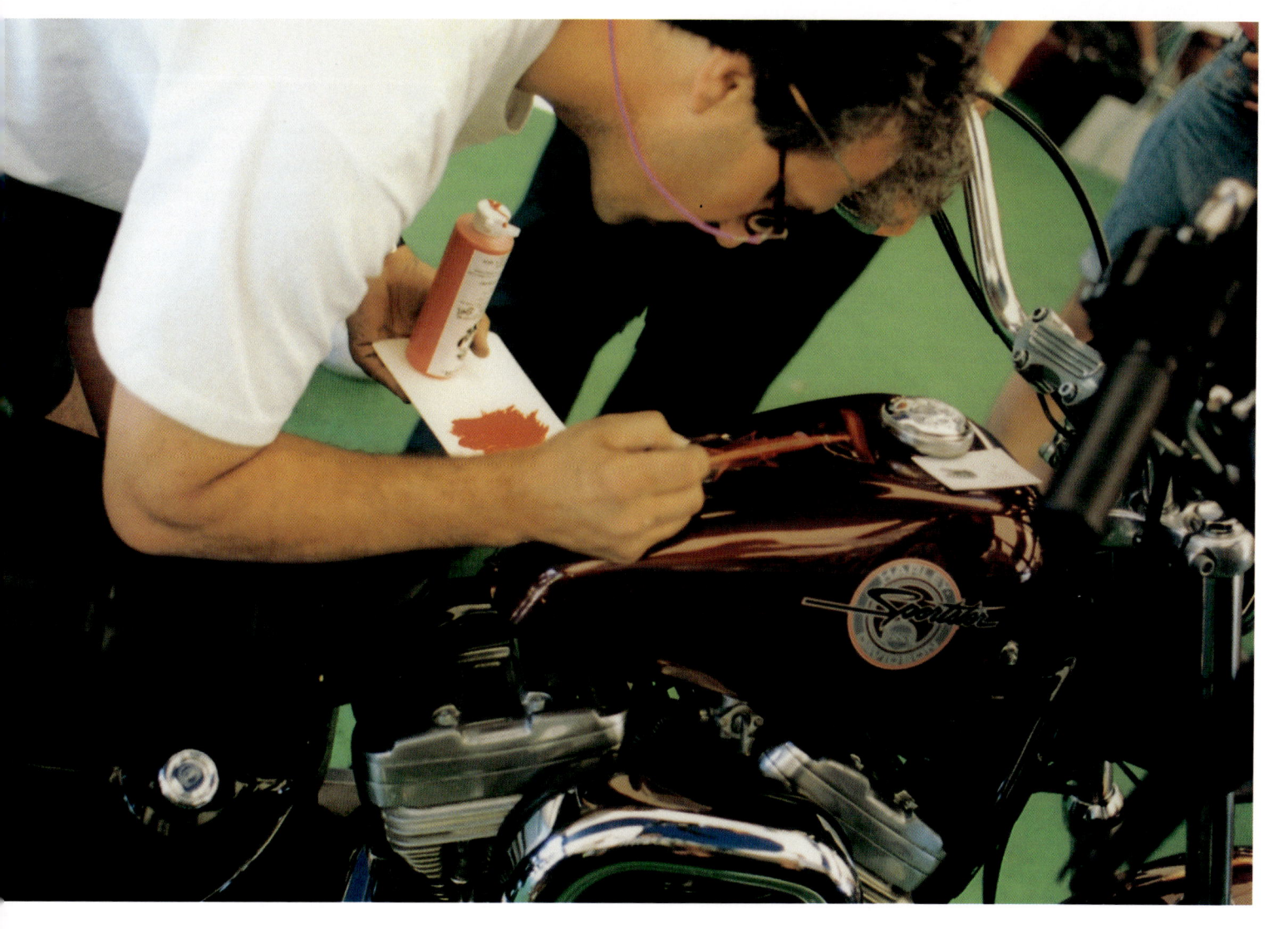

RESOURCE GUIDE

Sign Industry Publications

European Sign Magazine
Miller Freeman Technical
P.O. Box 325
3600 AH Maarssen
THE NETHERLANDS
Ph: 31 3465 54311
Fax: 31 3465 50372

Sign Builder Illustrated
Journalistic, Inc.
4095 Pine Cone Drive, Suite 2
Durham, NC 27707
Ph: (919) 489-1916

Sign Business
National Business Media, Inc.
1008 Depot Hill Office Park
Broomfield, CO 80020
Ph: (303) 469-0424
Fax: (303) 469-5730

SignCraft
SignCraft Publishing Co., Inc.
P.O. Box 60031
Ft. Meyers, FL 33906
Ph: (941) 939-4644
Fax: (941) 939-0607
Books on signmaking

Signs of the Times
ST Publications, Inc.
407 Gilbert Ave.
Cincinnati, OH 45202
Ph: (513) 421-2050
(800) 925-1110 (orders)
Fax: (513) 421-5144
Books on signmaking and screen printing

Signs of the Times en español
ST Publications, Inc.
407 Gilbert Ave.
Cincinnati, OH 45202
Ph: (513) 421-2050
Fax: (513) 421-5144

Vinyl Products

Vinyl Films

Arlon Adhesives and Film Div.
2811 S. Harbor Blvd.
Santa Ana, CA 92704
Ph: (800) 540-2811 (in CA)
Ph: (800) 854-0361 (out of state)
Fax: (714) 540-7190

Avery Dennison Marking & Promotional Films Div.
250 Chester St.
Painesville, OH 44077
Ph: (216) 639-3000
Fax: (216) 639-3759

Flexcon Co., Inc.
Flexcon Industrial Park
Spencer, MA 01562
Ph: (508) 885-3973
Fax: (508) 885-8400

MacTac
4560 Darrow Rd.
Stow, OH 44224
Ph: (216) 688-1111
Fax: (216) 688-2540

3M Commercial Graphics Div.
3M Center Bldg. 220-6W-06
St. Paul, MN 55144
Phone: (612) 733-1017
Fax: (612) 736-4233

Rexham Decorative
P.O. Box 800
Lancaster, SC 29721
Ph: (803) 285-4620

Ritrama Duramark
341 Eddy Rd.
Cleveland, OH 44108
Ph: (216) 851-2300
Fax: (216) 851-1938

Additional Vinyl Products

Arlon Adhesives and Films
2811 S. Harbor
P.O. Box 5260
Santa Ana, CA 92704
Ph: (714) 540-0361
Striping Products

Exciter's Graphics Supply
11555 D Ave.
Auburn, CA 95603
Ph: (916) 823-5197
Ph: (800) 886-5166
Fax: (916) 823-8239
Vinyl Tech Vinyl Coating Paints

Filmhandler
2000 Yolande Ave.
Lincoln, NE 68521
Ph: (402) 474-1243
Ph: (800) 336-3971
Fax: (402) 474-1361
Stainless Steel NT and OLFA knives and blades, Li'l Chiselers

Gerber Scientific Products, Inc.
151 Batson Drive
Manchester, CT 06040
Ph: (203) 643-1515
Fax: (203) 645-5645
Graphic design and production hardware
Software and materials
Gerber EDGE™ vinyl printer

GridView, Ltd.
4150 Industrial Drive
St. Peters, MO 63376
Ph: (800) 724-4743
Fax: (314) 926-7510
GridView Lettering and Layout Projection Guide

3M Automotive Trades Div.
3M Center Bldg. 223-6N-01
St. Paul, MN 55144
Ph: (800) 364-3577
Striping Products

Rapid Tac
186 Combs Dr.
Merlin, OR 97532
Ph: (800) 350-7751
Fax: (503) 474-9447

SpeedPress Tool Co.
11404 Sorrento Valley Road
#111
San Diego, CA 92121
Ph: (800) 647-7446
Fax: (619) 558-0587
SpeedPress Tool

Software

Computer Aided Sign Making Products

Alpha Merics Corp
4420 Shopping Lane
Simi Valley, CA 93063
Ph: (805) 520-3664
Fax. (805) 520-3665
Color-output product: Spectrum 5248 and Spectrum 5290

American Small Business Computers
1 American Way
Pryor, OK 74361
Ph. (918) 825-7555
Fax: (918) 825-6359
CAS Software: Vinyl CAD Professional Signmaking software

Amiable Technologies
Scott Plaza Two, Suite 625
Philadelphia, PA 19113
Ph: (610) 521-6300
Fax: (610) 521-0111
CAS Software, CAS Bridge Software

Anagraph, Inc.
3100 Pullman St.
Costa Mesa, CA 92626
Ph: (714) 540-2400
Fax: (714) 966-2400
CAS software and bridge software

Aries Graphics Intl.
5963 LaPlace Ct., Suite 110
Carlsbad, CA 92008
Ph: (800) 294-7273
Fax: (619) 929-0234
Sign Wizard signmaking machine and compatible software

Autogram Intl.
C/O Signprinters
1486 Max Dr.
Tallahasee, FL 32303
Ph: (904) 575-3828
Fax: (904) 575-4828
CAS software

Beacon Graphics Systems
10 County Line Rd., Suite 24
Somerville, NJ 08876
Ph: (800) 762-9205
Fax: (908) 231-8943
CAS software

Belcom Corp.
3135 Madison St.
Bellwood, IL 60104
Fax: (708) 544-5607
Color output product

Cactus
17 Industrial Rd.
Fairfield, NJ 07004
Ph: (201) 575-8810
Fax: (201) 575-5512
Color output product

Cadlink Technology Corp.
2440 Don Reid Dr., Suite 100
Ottawa, ON K1H 8H5
Canada
Ph: (800) 545-9581
Fax: (613) 247-1488

Calcomp
2411 West LaPalma Ave.
Anaheim, CA 92801
Ph: (800) 932-1212
Fax: (714) 821-2832
Color output product

Converter Solutions
Koberesteig 6
Berlin, 13156
GERMANY
Ph: 49 30 4827107
Fax: 49 30 4559977
CAS software and bridge software

Cybersign Ltd. Inc.
196 Boston Ave., Suite 2000
Medford, MA 02155
Ph: (617) 391-3100
Fax: (617) 393-0931
CAS software and bridge software

Encad
6059 Cornerstone Ct. West
San Diego, CA 92121
Ph: (619) 452-0882
Fax: (619) 452-0891
Color output product

Gerber Scientific Products
151 Batson Dr.
Manchester, CT 06040
Ph: (800) 222-7446
Fax: (203) 645-2479
CAS software and color output product

Infographic Technologies, Inc.
250 Williams St.
Atlanta, GA 30303
Ph: (404) 523-4944
Fax: (404) 523-4882
Color output product

Lasermaster Corp.
6900 Shady Oak Rd.
Eden Prairie, MN 55344
Ph: (800) 688-8342
Fax: (612) 944-1244
Color output product

3M Co. Commercial Graphics Div.
3M Center Bldg. 220-6W-06
St. Paul, MN 55144
Ph: (800) 328-3908
Fax: (612) 736-4233
Color output product: Scotchprint electronic graphic system

Metromedia Technologies
1320 N. Wilton Place
Los Angeles, CA 90028
Ph: (213) 856-6500
Fax: (213) 469-0843
Large scale digital imaging

Procut USA
3186 Airway Ave.
Costa Mesa, CA 92626
(714) 5409-7750
Fax: (714) 540-7556
CAS bridge software

Raster Graphics, Inc.
3025 Orchard Pkwy
San Jose, CA 95134
Ph: (800) 441-4788
Fax: (408) 232-4100
Color output product

Rocky Mountain Software
9739-63 Ave.
Edmonton, AB T6E 0G7
Canada
Ph: (403) 439-3303
Fax: (403) 439-3409
CAS bridge software

Scanvec, Inc.
155 West St.
Wilmington, MA 01887
Ph: (800) 866-6227
Fax: (508) 694-9482
CAS software and bridge software

Sign Equipment Engineering, Inc.
P.O. Box 6188
Bellevue, WA 98008
Ph: (206) 747-0693
Fax: (206) 562-3017
CAS software and bridge software

Sign Max Enterprises, Inc.
3705 Tricentenaire Blvd.
Montreal, QC H1B 5W3
Canada
Ph: (514) 644-3177
Fax: (514) 644-3173

Signtech USA, Ltd.
4669 Hwy. 90 West
San Antonio, TX 78237
Ph: (800) 353-9322
Fax: (210) 436-5711
Color output product

Softeam
3000 Chestnut Ave., Suite 108-A
Baltimore, MD 21211
Ph: (800) 305-8326
Fax: (410) 243-1259
CAS software and bridge software

Solustan, Inc.
165 Chestnut St. #200
Needham, MA 02192
Ph: (617) 449-7666
Fax: (800) 666-8789
CAS software and bridge software

Summagraphic
8500 Cameron Rd.
Austin, TX 78754
Ph: (800) 337-8662
Fax: (512) 873-1329
Color imaging product

Symbol Graphics
1047 W. 6th St.
Corona, CA 91720
Ph: (909) 736-4040
Fax: (909) 737-0652
CAS software

URW
4 Manchester St.
Nashua, NH 03060
Ph. (800) 229-8791
Fax: (603) 882-7210
CAS software

Visual Edge Technology, Inc.
306 Potrero Ave.
Sunnyvale, CA 94086
Ph: (408) 245-1100
Fax: (408) 245-1107
Color output product

Vutek, Inc.
P.O. Box 1546
Meredith, NH 03253
Ph: (603) 279-4635
Fax: (603) 279-6191
Color output product

Hardware and Cutting Plotters

Accupro Inc.
1011 Highway 22
W. Bldg. C, Box 8
Phillipsburg, NJ 08865
Ph: (908) 454-5998
Fax: (908) 454-1957

Allen Datagraph, Inc.
2 Industrial Way
Salem, NH 03079
Ph: (800) 258-6360
Fax: (603) 893-9042

Anagraphic, Inc.
3100 Pullman St.
Costa Mesa, CA 92626
Ph: (800) 942-4270
Fax: (714) 966-2400

Euro Tech Corp.
14823 E. Hindsdale Ave.
Englewood, CO 80112
Ph: (303) 690-9000
Fax: (303) 690-9010

Gerber Scientific Products
151 Batson Dr.
Manchester, CT 06040
Ph: (800) 222-7446
Fax: (203) 290-5794

Ioline Corp.
12020 113 Ave. NE
P.O. Box 97095
Kirkland, WA 98034
Ph: (800) 598-0029
Fax: (206) 823-8898

Mimaki Engineering Co. Ltd.
5-9-41 Kitashinagawa
Siniagawa-Ku
Tokyo 141
JAPAN
Ph: 81-3-5420-8671
Fax: 81-3-5420-8688

Mutoh America, Inc.
3007 E. Chambers St.
Phoenix, AZ 85040
Ph: (800) 445-8782
Fax: (602) 276-9007

Newing-Hall, Inc.
2019 Monroe St.
Toledo, OH 43624
Ph: (800) 521-2615
Fax: (800) 435-7131

New Hermes, Inc.
2200 Northmont Pkwy.
Duluth, GA 30136
Ph: (800) 843-7337
Fax: (800) 533-7637

Roland Digital Corp.
1961 McGaw Ave.
Irvine, CA 92714
Ph: (714) 975-0560
Fax: (714) 975-0569

Summagraphics Corp.
8500 Cameron Rd.
Austin, TX 78754
Ph: (800) 444-3245
Fax: (512) 835-1916

Vinyl Technologies
2 Omega Way
Littleton, MA 01460
Ph: (800) 836-8983
Fax: (508) 952-6036

Western Graphtec, Inc.
11 Vanderbilt
Irvine, CA 92718
Ph: (800) 654-7568
Fax: (714) 855-0895

Banner Products

Banner Cloth

Advertising Ideas, Inc.
3281 Barber Rd.
P.O. Box 473
Barberton, OH 44203
Ph: (216) 745-9444
Fax: (216) 745-6701

Banner Supply, Inc.
611 W. 22nd Ste. 1-A
Houston, TX 77008
Ph: (713) 802-2225
Fax: (713) 802-0008

Banner Factory 5777
3711 Beverly Blvd.
Los Angeles, CA 90004
Ph: (213) 664-8282
Fax: (213) 664-07987

Eastern Banner Supply
2582 Spring Lake Rd.
Mooresville, IN 46158
Ph: (317) 831-6055
Fax: (213) 831-9874

National Banner Co. Inc.
11938 Harry Hines Blvd.
Dallas, TX 75234
Ph: (214) 241-2131
Fax: (800) 468-0700

Banner Hems/Heat Sealed

Banner Factory 5777
3711 Belverly Blvd.
Los Angeles, CA 90004
Ph: (213) 664-8282
Fax: (213) 664-0798

ND Graphic Products Ltd.
4309 Steeles Ave. W.
Downsview, ON M3N 1V7
Canada
Ph: (416) 663-6416
Fax: (416) 663-6398

Banner Paper

ND Graphic Products Ltd.
4309 Steeles Ave. W.
Downsview, ON M3N 1V7
Canada
Ph: (416) 663-6416
Fax: (416) 663-6398

Royal Wholesale Banner
4660 Ironton St.
Denver, CO 80239
Ph: (303) 371-1200
Fax: (303) 371-3383

Screen Printing Products

(Includes screens, squeegees, clamps, cleaning and solvent recovery systems, and most other miscellaneous screen printing materials and supplies. Almost all screen printing supplies necessary will be available at your local or regional screen printing supply house. For additional information on screen printing materials and equipment, contact ST Publications, 407 Gilbert Ave., Cincinnati, OH 45202. (513) 421-2050, (800) 925-1110. Fax: (513) 421-5144. ST Publications publishes an annual *Screen Printing* Buyer's Guide.)

Majestech Corp.
Rt. 100, P.O. Box 440
Somers, NY 10589
Ph: (914) 232-7781
(800) 431-2200 (out of state)
Fax: (914) 232-4004

Tetko Inks Nazdar
1087 North Branch St.
Chicago, IL 60622
Ph: (312) 943-8338
(800) 736-7636
Fax: (312) 943-8215

Colonial Printing Ink Corp.
180 E. Union Ave.
East Rutherford, NJ 07073
Ph: (201) 933-6100
Fax: (201) 933-3361

Wood Products

Balsa Wood

Baltek Corp.
10 Fairway Ct. P.O. Box 195
Northvale, NJ 07647
Ph: (201) 767-1400
Fax: (201) 387-6631

Manufacturer of Foam Board

Coastal Enterprises
P.O. Box 487
Orange, CA 92613
Ph: (714) 771-4969
(800) 845-0745 (out of state)

Manufacturer of Precision Board

Sign Arts Products
P.O. Box 9573
Brea, CA 92622

Manufacturer of Sign Foam

Z-Tech
1305 Cedar
Lansing, MI 48910
Ph: (517) 482-1155
Fax: (517) 663-5035

Paint Products

Many of the materials used for the successful faux finisher are everyday household items. However, the Finishing School does act as a distributor of several items that are ideal to complete your faux finishing project. All of the following are available from The Finishing School, 334 Main St., Port Washington, NY 11050, (516) 767-6422: Water-based paints, faux effects products, cheesecloths, a new Munsell Color System Set which comes complete with a video series, books and videos. In addition to a series of videos, the Marxes are authors of the book, *Professional Painted Finishes*, which is also available from ST Publications, 407 Gilbert Ave., Cincinnati, OH 45202, (513) 421-2050, (800) 925-1110, Fax: (513) 421-5144.

Airbrushing Products

Airbrushes

Thayer & Chandler
28835 N. Herky Drive
Lake Bluff, IL 60044
Ph: (800) 548-9307
Fax: (708) 816-1356

Paasche Airbrush Co.
7440 W. Lawrence Ave.
Harwood Hts, IL 60656
Ph: (708) 867-9191
Fax: (708) 867-9198

Thomas Graphics
P.O. Box 3261
Orange, CA 92665
Ph: (800) 207-8051
Fax: (714) 282-7585

Medea Airbrush Products
P.O. Box 14397
Portland, OR 97214
Ph: (503) 253-7308
Fax: (503) 253-0721
(Iwata airbrushes)

Badger Air Brush Co.
9228 West Belmont Ave.
Franklin Park, IL 60131
Ph: (800) 57-BADGER

EFBE - The German Airbrush
Friedrich Boldt GMBH
Dieterichststrasse 35
AD-30159 Hanover
GERMANY
Ph: 49 511 32 34 20

Compressors

Silentaire Technology
7114 Rutland
Houston, TX 77009
Ph: (800) 972-7668
Fax: (713) 864-7314

Hyatt's Graphic Supply Co. Inc.
910 Main St.
Buffalo, NY 14202
Ph: (716) 884-8900

Paasche Airbrush Co.
7440 W. Lawrence Ave.
Harwood Hts, IL 60656
Ph: (708) 867-9191
Fax: (708) 867-9198

Exciter's Graphics Supply
11555 D Ave.
Auburn, CA 95603
Ph: (916) 823-5197
(800) 886-5166
Fax: (916) 823-8239

Carbon Dioxide Tanks

Hyatt's Grphic Supply Co. Inc.
910 Main St.
Buffalo, NY 14202
Ph: (716) 884-8900
Fax: (716) 884-3943

Airbrush Paint Manufacturers

Akzo Coatings Inc.
5555 Spalding Drive
Nocross, GA 30092
Ph: (404) 662-8464
Fax: (404) 662-5936

Aqual Flow/Hydra Color Systems
61 Maple Valley Drive
Carrollton, GA 30117
Ph: (404) 834-1013

Badger Air Brush Co.
9128 West Belmont
Franklin Park, IL
Ph: (708) 678-3104

Chroma Acrylics, Inc.
205 Bucky Drive
Lititz, PA 17543
Ph: (800) 257-8278

Consumers Paint Factory, Inc.
P.O. Box 6369
Gary, IN 46406
Ph: (219) 949-1684
Fax: 219) 9498-1612

Createx Colors
14 Airport Park Road
East Granby, CT 06026
Ph: (800) 243-2712
Fax: (203) 6543-0643

Decart, Inc.
P.O. Box 309
Marrisville, VT 06551
Ph: (802) 888-4217
Fax: (802) 888-4123

Golden Artists Colors, Inc.
Bell Road
New Berlin, NY 13411
Ph: (800) 959-6543
Fax: (607) 847-6767

HK Holbein, Inc.
P.O. Box 555
Williston, VT 05495
Ph: (802) 862-4573
Fax: (802) 658-5889

Hunt Manufacturing Co.
3 Commerce Square
2005 Market St.
Philadelphia, PA 19102
Ph: (215) 656-0300
Fax: (215) 656-3707

Ivy Imports, Inc.
12213 Distribution Way
Beltsville, MD 20705
Ph: (301) 595-0550
Fax: (301) 595-7868

Jack Richeson Co.
557 Marcella Drive
Kimberly, WI 54136
Ph: (800) 233-2404
Fax: (800) 233-2545

Koh-I-Noor
Grumbacher
100 North Street
Bloomsbury, NY 08804
Ph: (908) 479-4124
Fax: (800) 537-8939

Martin/F. Weber Co.
2727 Southampton Road
Philadelphia, PA 19154
Ph: (215) 677-5600
Fax: (503) 253-0721

Medea Co.
13585 NE Whitaker Way
Portland, OR 97230
Ph: (503) 253-7308
Fax: (503) 253-0721

Modern Masters
7340 Green Bush Ave.
North Hollywood, CA 91605
Ph: (818) 765-2915
Fax: (818) 765-0013

Salis International, Inc.
4093 North 28 Way
Hollywood, FL 33020
Ph: (305) 921-6961

Scooter Shooter
11611-M Salinaz
Garden Grove, CA 92643
Ph: (714) 636-6558

Siphon Art
P.O. Box 150710
San Rafael, CA 94915
Ph: (510) 236-0949

Tamiya America
2 Orion
Aliso Viejo, CA 92656
Ph: (800) 826-4922

Testos/Aztek
620 Buckbee Street
Rockford, IL 61104

Winsor & Newton
P.O. Box 1396
Piscataway, NJ 08852
Ph: (908) 562-5327

Cleaners

Medea Airbrush Procucts
P.O. Box 143976
Portland, OR 97214
Ph: (503) 253-7308
Fax: (503) 253-0721

Pinstriping Products

Brushes and Stripers

S. B. Beugler Co.
3667 Tracy St.
Los Angeles, CA 90039
Ph: (213) 664-2195
Fax: (213) 664-7757

Andrew Mack & Son. Brush Co.
225 E. Chicago
P.O. Box 157
Jonesville, MI 49250
Ph: (517) 849-9272
Fax: (517) 849-2251

Koh-I-Noor
Grumbacher
100 North Street
Bloomsbury, NY 08804
Ph: (908) 479-4124
Fax: (800) 537-8939

Striping Machines

S. B. Beugler Co.
3667 Tracy St.
Los Angeles, CA 90039
Ph: (213) 664-2195
Fax: (213) 664-7757

Newstripe, Inc.
1700 Jasper St.
Aurora, CO 80011
Ph: (303) 364-7786
Fax: (303) 364-7796

Tape

Anchor Continental, Inc.
2000 S. Beltline Blvd.
Columbia, SC 29205
Ph: (800) 845-2331
Fax: (800) 462-1293

C.P.F. A Division of Courtaulds Coatings
P.O. Box 6369
5300 W. 5th Ave.
Gary IN 46406
Ph: (219) 949-1684
Fax: (219) 949-1612

The Exciters
11555 D. Ave.
Auburn, CA 95603
Ph: (916) 823-6241
Fax: (916) 823-8239

Gregory, Inc.
200 S. Regler St.
P.O. Box 410
Buhler, KS 67522
Ph: (316) 543-6657
Fax: (316) 543-2690

Paint for Pinstriping

Akzo Nobile Coatings, Inc.
Chromatic Sign Finishes
5555 Spalding Drive
Norcross, GA 30092
Ph: (404) 662-8464
Fax: (404) 662-5936

C.P.F. A Division of Courtaulds Coatings
P.O. Box 6369
5300 W. 5th Ave.
Gary, IN 46406
Ph: (219) 949-1684
Fax: (219) 949-1612

Kurfees Coatings, Inc.
P.O. Box 1093
Louisville, KY 40201
Ph: (502) 584-0151
Ph: (800) 852-2661

Matthews Paint Co.
8201 100th St.
Kenosha, WI 53142
Ph: (419) 947-0700
Fax: (419) 947-0444

T. J. Ronan Paint Corp.
749 E. 135th St.
Bronx, NY 10454
Ph: (718) 292-1100
Fax: (718) 292-0406